Colonialism on the Margins of Africa

Colonial rule shaped the map of Africa like no other event in history. New borders were delineated; explorers and colonial armies were getting into the interior of the continent in order to grab the "magnificent cake of Africa."

Colonialism on the Margins of Africa examines less known and smaller or peripheral areas of Africa which played a significant role in the process of colonization of Africa by European powers. Due to diverse socio-economic, religious, ethno-linguistic, as well as political factors, places like the Somali-speaking territories, the Gambia, or Swaziland were divided between or surrounded by various administrative and political systems with different economic opportunities shaping the way to different futures in the post-colonial period.

This book will be of interest to students and scholars of African history and colonial and postcolonial politics.

Jan Záhořík is associate professor at the Department of Middle Eastern Studies, University of West Bohemia in Pilsen, Czech Republic.

Linda Piknerová is an assistant professor at the Department of Political Science and International Relations, University of West Bohemia in Pilsen, Czech Republic.

T0347746

Routledge Studies in the Modern History of Africa

This series includes in-depth research on aspects of economic, political, cultural and social history of individual countries as well as broad-reaching analyses of regional issues.

Themes include social and economic change, colonial experiences, independence movements, post-independence governments, globalization in Africa, nationalism, gender histories, conflict, the Atlantic Slave trade, the environment, health and medicine, ethnicity, urbanisation, and neo-colonialism and aid.

Colonialism on the Margins of Africa
Edited by Jan Záhořík and Linda Piknerová

Colonialism on the Margins of Africa

Edited by Jan Záhořík and Linda Piknerová

Routledge
Taylor & Francis Group

LONDON AND NEW YORK

First published 2018
by Routledge
2 Park Square, Milton Park, Abingdon, Oxon OX14 4RN

and by Routledge
605 Third Avenue, New York, NY 10017

First issued in paperback 2021

Routledge is an imprint of the Taylor & Francis Group, an informa business

© 2018 selection and editorial matter, Jan Záhořík and Linda Piknerová; individual chapters, the contributors

The right of Jan Záhořík and Linda Piknerová to be identified as the authors of the editorial material, and of the authors for their individual chapters, has been asserted in accordance with sections 77 and 78 of the Copyright, Designs and Patents Act 1988.

All rights reserved. No part of this book may be reprinted or reproduced or utilised in any form or by any electronic, mechanical, or other means, now known or hereafter invented, including photocopying and recording, or in any information storage or retrieval system, without permission in writing from the publishers.

Trademark notice: Product or corporate names may be trademarks or registered trademarks, and are used only for identification and explanation without intent to infringe.

British Library Cataloguing-in-Publication Data
A catalogue record for this book is available from the British Library

Library of Congress Cataloging-in-Publication Data
Names: Záhořík, Jan, 1979– editor, author. | Piknerová, Linda,
    1983– editor, author.
Title: Colonialism on the margins of Africa / edited by Jan Záhořík and
    Linda Piknerová.
Other titles: Routledge studies in the modern history of Africa.
Description: New York : Routledge, 2018. | Series: Routledge studies
    in the modern history of Africa | Includes bibliographical references
    and index.
Identifiers: LCCN 2017047012 | ISBN 9781138037946 (hardback) |
    ISBN 9781351710534 (e-book)
Subjects: LCSH: Africa—Colonial influence. | Africa—Colonization. |
    Africa—Politics and government—To 1945.
Classification: LCC DT31 .C57 2018 | DDC 325.6—dc23
LC record available at https://lccn.loc.gov/2017047012

ISBN 13: 978-0-367-78816-2 (pbk)
ISBN 13: 978-1-138-03794-6 (hbk)

Typeset in Times New Roman
by Apex CoVantage, LLC

Contents

vi *Contents*

Tables

Contributors

Jan Dvořáček is a historian from the University of Pardubice, whose interest lies in French colonial interests in the Horn of Africa.

Jakub Kydlíček is a historian, finishing his PhD in Modern History at the University of West Bohemia in Pilsen. His special focus is the colonial period in Maghreb, primarily Tunisia.

Linda Piknerová is an assistant professor at the Department of Political Science and International Relations, University of West Bohemia in Pilsen. She is a specialist in international relations, with a special focus on Southern African region. She has published several monographs on South Africa (in Czech).

Kateřina Rudincová is an Africanist/political geographer, serving as an assistant professor at the Department of Geography, Faculty of Sciences, Humanities and Education, Technical University of Liberec, Czech Republic. She has been dealing with the issues of human rights, right to self-determination, and colonial heritage in Africa, and has published several articles in the field.

Filip Strych is an Africanist/historian, currently finishing his PhD studies at the Department of History, University of West Bohemia in Pilsen, Czech Republic. He has published several articles on the history of the Senegambia, and China-Africa relations.

Jan Záhořík is an Africanist/historian, serving as associate professor at the Department of Middle Eastern Studies, University of West Bohemia in Pilsen, Czech Republic. He has published numerous articles and several monographs on the history and politics of the Horn of Africa, conflicts in Africa, and European-African relations.

Introduction

Jan Záhořík and Linda Piknerová

Colonialism in Africa has been subject of numerous monographs and studies in last century. Still, it remains an issue that causes a lot of controver-
sies and emotions. Except for Ethiopia and Liberia, European colonialism
spread its influence all over the continent; and Great Britain, France, Belgium, Portugal, Spain, Germany, and Italy divided newly formed territories among themselves. Historiography on colonial Africa is very wide and
almost endless, ranging from early accounts legitimizing the "civilizing
mission" to postcolonial critique of European colonial impact on Africa.
Colonial rule shaped the map of Africa like no other event in history. New
borders were delineated; explorers and colonial armies were getting into the
interior of the continent in order to grab the "magnificent cake of Africa."
A look at the map of Africa shows how a great variety of states in terms of
size, population, resources, and ethnic composition came into being after
the imposition of colonial rule on Africa: on one hand, there are enormous-
sized states with limited number of inhabitants, like Niger, Mali, Chad, Central African Republic, etc.; on the other hand, we can find very small states
of insignificant size including the Gambia, Swaziland, Rwanda, Burundi,
Djibouti. Some of the abovementioned states existed already long before the
European colonialism and were only incorporated under the colonial shelter.

Similarly significant (with direct psychological and physical impacts)
aspects of colonialism included various forms of oppression and violence,
manifested by suppression of anti-colonial West African (often Muslim)
revolts, elimination of the Herero rebellion in former German South-West
Africa, or clearly brutal behavior of colonial masters in Congo Free State
during Leopold II rule and race for rubber. On the other hand, African
states can be taken as successful, because despite all thinkable barriers and
obstacles, an African state is a functioning element, or together with Patrick
Chabal and Jean-Pascal Daloz, "Africa works."[1] Sure, creation of mostly
artificial borders did not respect existing social and cultural environment but
the emergence of ethnic identities is a process that started after the colonial

regimes were born. Most of the borders were simply delineated on tables of European governments as a result of the Berlin conference, 1884–1885. There cannot be any other solution than creation of artificial entities bringing many questions and a lot of unresolved problems.

One of such still visible today was a separation of speakers of one language into various colonies governed by different European power and thus having different administrative systems, languages of instruction, economic opportunities, jurisdictions, etc. Bakongo people can be taken as an example being divided into four colonies: French Congo, Belgian Congo, Angola, and Gabon.[2] Somali speaking peoples were divided into five completely different settings and administrative environments: Ethiopia, French Somaliland (Djibouti today), Italian Somalia, British Somaliland, and the British colony of Kenya. Social and political consequences of the Scramble for Africa have led to the growth of nationalist and separatist movements and tendencies that were legitimized by colonial past (Eritrea, Somaliland).

Every European power tried to develop its own administrative system and differed also in perception of Africans, though generally we can state that the tendency was to look upon an African as an inferior being. The Era of Imperialism, as the late stage of European colonialism is usually called (ca. 1870–1960), meant a true superiority of one society over another, its control, facilitated by technological lead of Europe.[3]

French colonial system based on a direct rule and direct control over the colonies suggested vast expenditures and energy spent on creation of massive administrative apparatus and involvement of French bureaucrats. Since the end of the nineteenth century, the French wanted to create an undisrupted Francophone territory that would connect Senegal with the Red Sea and Indian Ocean. When the British completed plans to connect Cairo with Cape Town, the French were blocked and there was an almost clash of both armies at Fashoda (1898) in what is now Sudan.[4]

Strategy of the French was based on strengthening of political and cultural dominance in all spheres of African life and society. Due to a long-lasting Anglo-French rivalry and international political and economic superiority of Great Britain, the program of the French colonial policy became a "cultural export" based on assimilation, i.e., spread of French language and culture in newly conquered territories. A part of this was a strategy to educate "loyal" African political elites in order to keep continuity of French dominance in emancipating colonies after the World War II. First presidents of independent African Francophone countries were thus close friends of France and spent at least part of their lives in Paris. Here we can place for instance the first Senegalese President Léopold Sédar Senghor, first President of Côte d'Ivoire Félix Houphouët-Boigny or the first President of Niger, Hamani Diori.[5]

The idea of unification of Francophone colonies in Africa via linguistic and cultural assimilation had to prevent these countries from disintegration experienced by some of the Portuguese of Belgian colonies in the era of early independence. Strong patrimonial relation of the colonial metropole to its colonies was largely manifested by de Gaulle's government unwillingness to allow any visible liberalization or emancipating mechanisms due to fears of chaotic and quick decolonization. The example of Guinea that voted for independence in 1958 in a referendum offered by France, or of Algeria, which in a French collective memory was considered a part of France on Africa soil, show how worried Paris was of losing its power and prestige including economic and cultural significance in Africa. Despite this fact we cannot overestimate French cultural imperialism as only some 15% of people in Francophone Africa speak French while the rest of the population gives preference to local languages.[6]

The British, unlike the French, utilized the system of indirect rule that did not rely on such financial efforts but obviously affected lives of individuals in the same manner. This was remarkable primarily in "pearls of the British Empire" such as Kenya or Nigeria. However, unlike the French, the Brits did not have any desire to assimilate Africans.[7] They allowed Africans many of their traditional institutions as the main aim was economic profit, not cultural dominance. British, or generally European colonialism, owed much to great explorers and personalities such as Cecil Rhodes who in fact established the basis of British imperialism in South Africa. North Rhodesia, named after him, soon became one of the most important components of the British Empire. The richest area was the region along borders with former Belgian Congo that came into being as Copper Belt due to vast deposits of copper and other minerals.

The manuscript "Colonialism on the margins of Africa" deals with less known and smaller or peripheral areas of Africa which were, however, influenced by colonial rule with the same intensity as the rest of the continent. Nevertheless, while there exist a large amount of books and studies related to comparative colonial studies in general, only few things were written in regard to the subject-matter. Moreover, these are rarely comparative in its nature, so we may find a number of books written in French dealing with its colonial past, for instance in Djibouti,[8] a few pieces regarding the colonial history of the Gambia,[9] or several monographs concerning small landlocked states of Lesotho and Swaziland.[10] The Horn of Africa (represented by three chapters in this volume) is a specific case itself. Primarily, Ethiopia has never been colonized by any European power (except for a short-lived Italian occupation in 1936–1941). Second, Ethiopia itself is being characterized as a colonial power side by side with France, Great Britain, and Italy. Due to very turbulent political development in Ethiopia in last century, its past is still a matter of political as well as academic debates.[11] As can be seen, there exist a certain void or at least some space in examining and analyzing colonial history in Africa especially in its 'marginal' and 'marginalized' territories which we are tending to explore. A comparative and multidisciplinary view will enable us to find patterns as well as differences in colonial heritage and colonial approaches to the studied territories.

The book deals with specific African territories and states that belong to geographically rather smaller entities but played a significant role in the process of colonization of Africa by European powers. Due to diverse socio-economic, religious, ethno-linguistic, as well as political environment, places like the Somali-speaking territories, the Gambia, or Swaziland were divided between or surrounded by various administrative and political systems with different economic opportunities shaping the way to different future(s) in post-colonial period. The monograph composed of several case studies examines geographical, socio-economic, ethnic, religious, and international contexts of these territories and analyzes the influence of colonialism on their post-colonial existence. While we do have general information and sufficient survey of larger units, forms of colonial systems and influence of colonialism on various African states such as Angola, Mali, Kenya, or Algeria, smaller states such as Djibouti, the Gambia, or Lesotho still face minimal interest of scholarly community and therefore, it is of vital need to fill this gap by examining their colonial past in interdisciplinary perspective including history, anthropology, international relations, and political geography.

Each chapter deals not only with different territory or area, but at the same time focuses on a little different aspect of colonial rule or colonial discourse. Chapters thus deal with issues such as nationalism, indigenous versus foreign forms of colonialism, colonial imagination, colonial economy, the issue of colonial boundaries, etc. The main arguments of the book are that despite a lower strategic importance of these 'peripheral' areas for European colonialists, these smaller territories played equally important roles as compared to their bigger neighbors due to a number of factors which will be discussed in the chapters listed below. The issue is not only to shed some new light on formation, rise and fall of colonial regimes in Africa (like in the case of the Gambia), but also to debate some politically sensitive current issues including the alleged Ethiopian colonialism versus indigenous groups of what is now Ethiopia that may have (and do have) a serious impact on the shape and form of academic discourse in last couple of decades. Therefore, we are convinced that the book will find its place on the market as it will be useful (not only) for students and academic interested in colonial history of Africa, comparative history in general, political geography, as well as in the history of particular areas included in the book.

The first chapter, written by Jan Záhořík, gives an account on Ethiopia and the colonial discourse related to this country. Colonialism in Africa is somewhat automatically related to European domination that was marked by the Scramble for Africa. At the end of the nineteenth century, almost the whole continent was divided between European powers such as Great Britain, France, Portugal, Spain, Italy, Germany, and Belgium. Since that time, African states have always been discussed in regard to their colonial legacies and consequent postcolonial issues including ethnic and religious rivalries, border disputes, separatism, nationalism, authoritarianism, or socio-economic challenges. When considering colonial past, Ethiopia usually stands alone as a unique example of an African society that was able to defeat a European power and thus maintain its independence, at least in territorial sense. However, Ethiopia itself was a political unit, like any other, that in previous centuries was constantly changing the size of its territory in regard to foreign threats and internal challenges. The most turbulent period occurred in the second half of the nineteenth century which brought Ethiopia into an era of territorial expansion southwards, westwards, and eastwards to a landscape that was not conquered by any foreign power and thus enjoyed relative independence being composed of multiple societies.

In the second chapter, Kateřina Rudincová deals with the Great Imperial Game in the Horn of Africa and Its Impact on Current Political Processes in Somalia. Towards the end of fifteenth century, the Somali-speaking territories were partitioned by colonial powers as Great Britain, Italy, France, and regional power Ethiopia. Differences between British indirect rule in northern Somalia and Italian direct rule in the South had their impacts on the further development of united Somali Republic since it was very difficult to create one state entity from the territories with different colonial past and inherited political, judicial, and economic systems. Currently, differences in colonial systems are used by the political representation of Somaliland as a part of its legitimization strategies to achieve independent existence. Inclusion of traditional elders during the British colonial rule in contrast to the direct Italian administration caused the transformation of Somali political systems and societies and influenced different forms of peace negotiations in Somaliland and southern Somalia. The chapter will deal with the impact of colonial partition and the creation of colonial boundaries on further political developments in Somalia. The special attention will be paid to the impact of different colonial administrations to differences of the current peace initiatives in Somaliland in contrast to the southern Somalia.

In the third chapter Jan Dvořáček and Jan Záhořík analyze the Importance of Djibouti for economy and politics in the Horn of Africa. For decades, the Horn of Africa has attracted the attention of world powers, especially for its strategic position on the geopolitical map that enabled to control the important space in the Middle East and in the Indian Ocean. Since the opening of the Suez canal, the whole region became one of the most important sea waterways connecting European, African, and Asian trade. French colonial activities in the Horn started in this period and culminated with the construction of a strategic railway Djibouti-Addis Abeba. All above-mentioned aspects played very significant role in decolonization time. Belated independence of the sea port Djibouti caused tensions in French-Ethiopian relations that were extremely complicated after the independence of Somalia, whose territorial claims had intensified in 1960. The chapter deals with specific position of small French territory which became the last continental colony in Sub-Saharan Africa. The main focus will be concentrated on economic, political, and ethnic environment of Djibouti in the time of high geopolitical tensions in Africa.

In the fourth chapter, Filip Strych focuses on the Gambia between French and British Interests and discusses Colonial Heritage and Post-Colonial Realities. There is only small amount of papers focused on the history of the former British Colony the Gambia. Those works are focused on various types of trades (i.e., groundnut trade, slave trade) or the political history of this region. This chapter examines the official reports from Bathurst (now Banjul), the capital situated on the St. Mary's Island, to London. Those reports provide a detailed insight into the strategy of the Great Britain. The case study will use an analysis of the letters originally stored in the National Archives in Kew, London. The ongoing output will be how the governors understood the colony and protectorate in general, how they handled the local rulers, merchants, local people, etc. The analysis will help to understand how the Colonial Office influenced the official administration in the Gambia. Those observations will be synthetized then into a few major parts: the real influence of the Colonial Office, the statements of the administration in the Gambia, and the interactions between the administration and local people.

Jakub Kydlíček in the fifth chapter gives an insight into French images of the French Protectorate in Tunisia based on the study of travelers' accounts from the end of the nineteenth century. The chapter is focused on images of the French protectorate in Tunisia since 1881. Although much commentators' attention had been focused on Algeria's status within *"francophonie,"* we use archives from neighboring Tunisia from the late nineteenth century. Traveler's records and remarks as micro-historical evidences can serve as good as ethnographical material or archive records. In this chapter, the core is to create an inventory of the most often mentioned themes and topics among travelers and re-examine them by using archive documents of the Protectorate administration. The research question is how an ideological background of the French "mission civilisatrice" was set into life and local micro-level of social interactions. By combining archive documentation and traveler's observations, we try to point out some findings about the protectorate administration practices and their relationships with the local "indigénes" people. As the indigenous sources and material that could cover the sight of the local Arabs and Berbers is mostly missing, we rely mostly on oral history evidences. Thus we can at least reconstruct the rough frame of the societies that came under French rule after the creation of the protectorate administration apparatus. As we cannot describe the entire period of the "Régence" in Tunisia, we choose the very beginnings (ca. 1880–1914) as the target for examination. The choice is not casual – even in few decades after the establishment of the French domination, reactions among France-based intellectuals and personalities influenced the public opinion, and some of its influences are reflected by travelers and visitors in the Protectorate. The second aspect of the specification of research area is the territory. Relatively small attention has been paid for the remote and desolate areas in the South of (modern) Tunisia, therefore the study is focused mostly on the governorate Arad (today's Gabes district).

Ruanda-Urundi, former German colony, became a Belgian mandated territory after the World War I and Belgium administered both countries up until 1962. As Jan Záhořík shows in the sixth chapter, control over migration of labor force was one of the main tasks of Belgian administrative as both Eastern Congo and Ruanda-Urundi were territories important either for agriculture or mining. Migration occurred both spontaneously or as a forced and regulated movement of people, which also included migration to British colonial territories. The author gives an account in the recruitment process and the reasons and causes of labor migration from colony to another.

In Chapter 7, Linda Piknerová focuses on two small territories in Southern Africa, namely Swaziland and Lesotho, as they were Surrounded by Boer and Apartheid Reality. The chapter focuses on two landlocked countries influenced by imperial policies of two European powers (Great Britain and Portugal) for many years. Besides the penetration of European powers, both kingdoms had to face imperial ambitions of two Boer states – Transvaal (South African Republic) and Orange spreading its influence across the region since the second part of nineteenth century. Although both Boer states had been defeated by two British colonies and annexed by the British Empire, a Boer element remained one of the significant features determining the existence of both monarchies. Due to the threat of Boer expansion, Lesotho and Swaziland were incorporated into British Empire, and British rule became one of the crucial points defining the modern political life until the 1960s when both states became independent. However both newly reestablished monarchies had to face apartheid regime established after the World War II in the Republic of South Africa, which tried to affect political reality in both states in many perspectives. Political, geopolitical, or security questions can be mentioned as the main challenges resulting from the presence of apartheid regime. Thus, post-colonial reality still remained caught by the external factors arising from the non-democratic reality in the Republic of South Africa.

Notes

1 Patrick Chabal and Jean-Pascal Daloz, *Africa Works: Disorder as Political Instrument* (Oxford: Oxford University Press, 1999).
2 Adu Boahen, *African Perspectives on Colonialism* (Baltimore: Johns Hopkins University Press, 1990), 96.
3 Jason Springhall, *Decolonization Since 1945* (New York: Palgrave Macmillan, 2001), 19.
4 Bruce Vandervort, *Wars of Imperial Conquest in Africa 1830–1914* (London and New York: Routledge, 1998), 178–183.
5 Patrick Manning, *Francophone Sub-Saharan Africa 1880–1995* (Cambridge: Cambridge University Press, 1998).
6 Ibid.
7 Paul Nugent, *Africa Since Independence* (New York: Palgrave Macmillan, 2004), 13.
8 See e.g. Simon Imbert-Vier, *Tracer des frontières à Djibouti* (Paris: Karthala, 2011).
9 See e.g. Arnold Hughes and David Perfect, *A Political History of the Gambia, 1816–1994* (Rochester: University of Rochester Press, 2008).
10 See e.g. Philip Bonner, *Kings, Commoners, and Concessionaires: The Evolution and Dissolution of the Nineteenth-Century Swazi State* (Cambridge: Cambridge University Press, 2002).
11 See e.g. John Markakis, *Ethiopia: The Last Two Frontiers* (Woodbridge: James Currey, 2011); Seyoum Hameso and Mohammed Hassen (eds.), *Arrested Development in Ethiopia* (Trenton: Red Sea Press, 2006); Tsega Etefa, *Integration and Peace in East Africa: A History of the Oromo Nation* (New York: Palgrave Macmillan, 2013).

1 Ethiopia and the colonial discourse

Jan Záhořík

Introduction

Colonialism in Africa is somewhat automatically related to the European domination that was marked by the Scramble for Africa. At the end of the nineteenth century, almost the whole continent was divided between European powers such as Great Britain, France, Portugal, Spain, Italy, Germany, and Belgium. Since that time, African states have always been discussed in regard to their colonial legacies and consequent postcolonial issues including ethnic and religious rivalries, border disputes, separatism, nationalism, authoritarianism, or socio-economic challenges.

When considering the colonial past, Ethiopia usually stands alone as a unique example of an African society that was able to defeat a European power and thus maintain its independence, at least in territorial sense. However, Ethiopia itself was a political unit, like any other, that in previous centuries was constantly changing the size of its territory in regard to foreign threats and internal challenges.[1] The most turbulent period occurred in the second half of the nineteenth century, which brought Ethiopia into an era of territorial expansion southwards, westwards, and eastwards to a landscape that was not conquered by any foreign power and thus enjoyed relative independence.[2] Ethiopia's territory, however, was a matter of constant changes and modifications throughout centuries, and the nineteenth century was not different. Non-Christian, Islamic, and other areas inhabited by dozens of societies speaking numerous languages began to be continuously incorporated into the Ethiopian Empire, at that time known as Abyssinia.

In the twentieth century, historical research on Ethiopia became politicized due to the nineteenth-century expansion of the Ethiopian Empire. Harold Marcus, one of the most prominent historians and scholars on Ethiopia, once began one of his papers with the following words: "The primacy of politics in Africa has led to serious distortions of the historical record, nowhere more evident than in Ethiopian studies. The misrepresentation commenced with the student activism of the 1960s."[3] It is true that since the period of revolutionary changes in Ethiopia we can observe a change in interpretation of Ethiopian history and its politicization. This chapter thus focuses on the so-called colonial discourse in regard to modern history of Ethiopia and how this discourse changes and perhaps complicates our understanding of the Ethiopian past. Moreover, it can also show us how the past is influencing the present in academic debates over the Ethiopian history.

Ethiopian history is a history of cultural interaction, religious diversity, conquests, migrations, integration, and assimilation. Still, the most politically sensitive debates occur along Amhara-Oromo line, as if these are some two homogeneous blocs. From the sixteenth century, the Oromo people began to migrate to the Ethiopian Highlands and settle in such diverse areas as Wellegga, Gojjam, and Wällo. In the following centuries, the process of assimilation and integration began as the Oromo interacted not only with the Ethiopian state, but primarily with their neighboring societies, where multiple languages were spoken. Even today, the modern history of Ethiopia, as well as of the Oromo people, remains a subject of sensitive debate, politicized opinions, and numerous publications of varying degrees of quality. While some authors (or, to be more accurate, political activists) tend to portray Oromo history as the history of a unified nation, fighting for centuries in order to gain independence from the Ethiopian Empire, more erudite scholars usually provide a more balanced picture of the turbulent developments in what is now Ethiopia.[4] First of all, Oromo society is divided into numerous groups and sub-groups, such as the Macha, the Tulama, the Arsi, and the Guji. In the nineteenth century, there existed several Oromo monarchies, mainly in South-West Ethiopia. The monarchies competed with each other and with their neighbors.[5] These groups lived in different ecological and social settings, religious environments, and political units; in some cases, they fought each other. Therefore, it is nearly impossible to perceive the history of the Oromo people (as is also the case of other peoples) as the history of a homogeneous unit. The same goes with any other ethnic group in what is now Ethiopia. Furthermore, Ethiopia is also a country of religious diversity, and religion has certainly played a very important role in last centuries crossing "real" or "alleged" ethnic lines. As shown by various authors, religion is challenging ethnic identity and changing relationships in many parts of Ethiopia.[6]

Ethiopia's modernization period

While the end of the nineteenth century was marked by enormous territorial expansion, the first decades of the twentieth century saw Ethiopia in the modernization period.[7] The late nineteenth century was also characterized by territorial expansion of Ethiopia and the quest for hegemony in the Horn of Africa that included several European powers (Italy, France, Great Britain). Expansion of Ethiopian territory into South, West, and East of what is now Ethiopia was a successful military event that until nowadays serves as one of the main problems of Ethiopian history. The question that many scholars tend to raise is "Was Ethiopia a colonial power?" and "Shall Ethiopia be decolonized?"

Mixing the idea of modernization with biblical ethos and ancient heritage combined with religious clash between Orthodox Christians on one hand and Muslims and pagans on the other, the so-called Abyssinian Empire saw itself as the main hegemony in the Horn of Africa.[8] Sudan, a neighbor to Ethiopia, played a similar role, trying to gain hegemony in the region. Both states were based on centralization and historical legitimacy, either Christian or Muslim. However, both were far from homogeneous in terms of ethnicity and religion.

While the Sudan under the Mahdists was a relatively short-lived entity, Ethiopia became a rival to European powers in the Horn of Africa and especially two events gained her an image of an exceptional unit in the "black continent." Historically, it was the victorious battle of Adowa in 1896 that brought Ethiopia on the map of the modern world and into the forefront of foreign interest at least for a short period of time.[9] Secondly, the Italian invasion to Ethiopia in 1935 and the subsequent war of 1935–1936 put Ethiopia into the category of a victim that had to face militarized, violent aggressor destroying a peaceful land of ancient civilization. Ethiopia resonated strongly especially among the African-American community in the United States and, according to Aric Putnam, was "reinvented as a figure of racially heterogeneous community, a community bound together through shared experience in political and mythical time."[10]

Each of these two events showed Ethiopia as opposed to European colonialism and thus to colonialism as such as this historical period was marked by dominance of a few European powers over large parts of non-European world, primarily Africa. However, it has established Ethiopia as a regional power dominated by Abyssinian elites who were, in the twentieth century, labeled by nationalist authors as "oppressive," "racist," or "terrorist" while promoting the idea of a "White, Christian, ethnocentric, occidental hegemonic power."[11]

Ethiopia, European powers, and expansionism

The year 1855 is usually taken as the beginning of (re)unification process of the Ethiopian state. The word *(re)unification* itself causes the same troubles as the word *colonialism* in regard to Ethiopia. Some scholars claim that there was no unified state before 1855 so we can hardly speak about reunification. Others have an opposite opinion and use the word reunification to describe the process of stabilization of the state fragmented during the period of *zemane mesafint* (the Era of Princes) in 1769–1855. Already in the nineteenth century, European travelers began to explore the Ethiopian Highlands and encounter local people, customs, habits, and languages. Ethiopia had an image of a noble country "in the possession of the Christians of Eastern Africa [that] is blessed with a climate that may, perhaps, challenge a comparison with any in the world."[12] However, beyond the core of the Ethiopian state, disunity was rather prevalent and occasional revolts against the state occurred primarily in Southern Ethiopia, where peasants were not so well armed but still resisted the pressure from the landowners.[13]

There are, obviously, manifold ways in which Ethiopian history is portrayed but two main branches of academic discourse compete with each other. The first can be called *statist* and perceives the history of Ethiopia as a history of united territory with all its shortcomings, advantages, and disadvantages, historical wins and losses, victims and winners, rights and wrongs. The second branch can be called an *anti-state discourse* which sees Ethiopia as an enemy to ethno-nationalist aspirations, as an oppressor ruled by one group of the rest of population, as a colonial power comparable to other colonial powers like France, Italy, Great Britain, etc.[14] The first gives attention to unification processes and positive developments in Ethiopia while the second is devoted to the study of "suffering," "inferiority," "subjugation," and "negative stereotypes" that accompany Ethiopian historiography ever since.[15]

The decisive point was the socialist revolution in 1974 which completely changed mentality and curriculum of Ethiopian schools and students who were then taught to hate the state because it was based on rotten feudal roots which put diverse ethnic groups into categories of second-class citizens at best.[16] However, this was the result of a long process that had its roots already in the 1950s and 1960s at the latest when students from Ethiopia began to travel abroad where they gained (beside other things) Marxist education. The rise of Marxism coincides with the development of nationalist movements in Africa. Despite many differences between Ethiopia and the rest of Africa (under colonial rule), several similarities can be found. For instance, many of the nationalist movements in Africa began as student movements or were formed around the workers' and trade unions, teachers and student associations. Primarily in West Africa, the situation after the World War II led to a continuous development of the middle-class, educated elites, allowed the young generation to study in Europe and gain education outside the country in order to contribute to the socio-economic development of its homeland after their return. French colonialism after the war was based on creation of 'Europeanized' Africa with a modern African working class as a crucial element.[17] Before 1941, education in Ethiopia was conducted in

French language and many Ethiopians studied in France and thus it was no surprise that for many young Marxist intellectuals in Ethiopia, the French Revolution served at least as an inspiration. New elites of intellectuals saw in Marxism "a principled way to reject the West that had supported Haile Selassie and hence Ethiopia's backwardness."[18]

Past and present

As can be seen so far, the discourse on modern history of Ethiopia is strongly influenced by politicization, accent on ethnicity, and idealization of the past in various contexts and backgrounds. But how can we distinguish between what is our genuine understanding of the past and what is the idealized understanding of the past?[19]

As examined by several authors, expansion of the Ethiopian state into territories south from what is now Addis Ababa had very different intensity and were undertaken in diverse areas against diverse populations or enemies. As retold by some, many of the people that were conquered by the Abyssinian military forces, simply lacked any kind of coherence including the Oromo (then pejoratively labeled as the Galla tribes), who were "rarely united since they were unfriendly with each other."[20] Such accounts can be observed in many primary materials written by mostly European observers.[21] The Oromo people form a significant part of Ethiopian society and thus an important part of Ethiopia's history. Since the sixteenth century, they have been known to the broader public as the people who migrated to the Ethiopian Highlands during and after the famous Ahmad Gragn invasion of the central part of what is now Ethiopia. This historical event changed the historical development of the Ethiopian Highlands and helped to establish the Oromo population as a significant, powerful, and decisive force.[22] Later, in the nineteenth century, many Oromo political units/states came into being, such as those of the Gibe region, including, for instance, Jimma Abba Jifar and Limmu Ennarea.

The so-called Oromo invasion of the Ethiopian Highlands also contributed to the much diversified linguistic setting we see in today's Ethiopia. The Oromo language is spoken by some thirty million people (both by native and second language speakers) and Oromo culture is an important part of Ethiopia's cultural heritage. In this regard, many Oromo institutions have come into existence during the past couple of decades and hundreds of books in the Oromo language are now in the process of being published in Ethiopia. As frequently stated, the most active element in these developments has been the Oromo diaspora, with its long list of authors involved in promoting Oromo history, culture, and society and, more generally, the history of the Ethiopian state.

What we see in contemporary clash over the interpretation of Ethiopian history, is to a certain sense a quarrel between social constructivism and essentialism. This can well be documented on many examples, for instance, now famous and unique collective volume called *Being and Becoming Oromo*,[23] which brought together wide range of authors from different disciplines and with various backgrounds. It clearly shows how different an understanding and a research of Ethiopian history can be, and how difficult is to find a unifying arguments. Needless to say that the book has been criticized as well as praised since it was published.[24]

According to Crawford Young, the naturalization of a territorial nation is a necessary prerequisite for the construction and maintenance of the integrity of the African state because within these states dozens of different societies have shared, due to the artificial creation of borders, the same territory but have not shared a common national mythology.[25] Only a few African states have a shared pre-colonial history and thus a consciousness of national integrity, namely Morocco, Egypt, and Ethiopia. Some other states at least evoke an historical existence going beyond the borders of colonialism (Botswana, Swaziland, Lesotho, Tunisia, Madagascar). Of course, in the context of politicized historiography in Ethiopia, any authors would question Young's premise of the national integrity of Ethiopia as it is regarded by many of the Oromo scholars as a colonial domain in which the Oromo (and other people) belong to the oppressed and thus have no national attachment.

In last couple of decades, a new wave of scholars, coming mostly from the Ethiopian diaspora, more specifically Oromo, blame the Ethiopian state of committing genocide on the Oromo people and other societies inhabiting the areas conquered by Abyssinians. While earlier Abyssinian historiography focused on greatness of Imperial courts and their successes, and considered other societies in the neighborhood enemies, at least some of contemporary scholars use the same static language in order to distinguish between Abyssinians and the Oromos or other non-Semitic people. The problem of studying the Ethiopian past thus lies in transferring our current knowledge and ideas of nationalism, ethno-nationalism, and colonialism into the era of more than one hundred years ago without proper understanding of the dynamics of political, social, economic, and international developments in the studied areas. Simplifications and accusations are the main characteristics of these materials. A good example can be given here:

> Ethiopian racism and White racism have conveniently intermarried in the U.S. policy formulation and implementation in Ethiopia. When policy issues are discussed on Ethiopia Semitic civility, Christianity, antiquity, bravery, and patriotism of Amharas and Tigrayans are

retrieved to valorize and to legitimize Habasha dominance and power. Moreover, the barbarism, backwardness, and destructiveness of Oromos and others are reinvented to keep Oromos and others from access to state power.[26]

In other words, the Ethiopian elites and the ruling classes have always been centered around the dominant lineages that were mostly Amharas, or Tigrayans, or of mixed origin. Furthermore, we cannot perceive the history of Ethiopia through ethnic lenses because of one simple reason: ethnic identities, ethno-nationalist movements, and political parties representing ethnic groups in Ethiopia are new, young, and fresh (in historical terms) while in the nineteenth century and earlier, we can hardly speak about modern ethnic identities in our contemporary understanding. As rightly pointed by Lahra Smith, not "only is there a multiplicity of visions of Ethiopian citizenship, there is diversity in the vision of Oromo political identity that represents the richness of human expression, both individual and group based."[27] When considering the Ethiopian past, one simply cannot perceive it through current (meaning ethnic in this sense) lenses although even nowadays the importance of ethnic identity itself is challenged by other crucial factors in Ethiopian society, primarily religion.[28] For instance, to claim that the Abyssinian state or Amharas themselves were oppressing the Oromo people can be seen as exaggeration at best. First of all, Ethiopia was ruled by Amharic speaking elites who had no contact with the rest of Amharic-speaking population inhabiting the Ethiopian Highlands.[29] Second, just as an Amhara ethnic identity is a recent phenomenon, the idea of Oromo identity going back centuries ago is far from reality as the Oromo did not unite as a single political unit at least until the end of the nineteenth century. The reason was simple, there existed many clans and political units speaking Oromo language but inhabiting vast and diverse areas from Wälläga to Harar, from Wällo to Moyale. Some of the Oromo groups "altered their ethnic markers and attributes, such as language, dialect, religion, mode of production, social structure, political system and customs."[30]

Conclusion

The process of state-building and nation-building in Ethiopia, as we can see, has been characterized by different context and settings than in the rest of Africa influenced by European colonial rule. However, due to specific nature of the Ethiopian state and its expansionist period at the end of the nineteenth century, the colonial discourse entered Ethiopia with perhaps even greater intensity than in the rest of Africa. The reasons for this lie in different perspectives on modern history of Ethiopia, politicization of ethnicity and primacy of ethnic identity in historical research. Therefore, even in a country which lacks any experience with European colonialism, the colonial discourse can play a significant part not only in historiography but in public and political debates in general. Contrary to the rest of Africa, in this case the issue of decolonization can hardly be materialized as the necessary question emerges: whom to decolonize from what? Accent on colonial nature of the Ethiopian state also complicates further debates concerning democratization of the society and politics, because colonialism has its ending in decolonization which gets us back to our previous question. However, with politicization of ethnicity and prevailing Marxist and essentialist views on Ethiopian history, it is probable that the colonial discourse will remain as one of the most significant features of contemporary debates over the nature of the Ethiopian state.

Notes

1 See e.g. Donald Crummey, *Land and Society in the Christian Kingdom of Ethiopia: From the Thirteenth to the Twentieth Century* (Urbana and Chicago: University of Illinois Press, 2000), or Mordechai Abir, *Ethiopia and the Red Sea: The Rise and Decline of the Solomonic Dynasty and Muslim-European Rivalry in the Region* (London: Frank Cass and Company, 1980).
2 See e.g. Bahru Zewde, *A History of Modern Ethiopia, 1885–1991* (Oxford: James Currey, 2001); R. H. Kofi Darkwah, *Shewa, Menelik and the Ethiopian Empire 1813–1889* (London: Oxford University Press, 1975); Sven Rubenson, *The Survival of Ethiopian Independence* (Addis Ababa: Kuraz Publishing Agency, 1991).
3 Harold G. Marcus, "The Corruption of Ethiopian History," in: *Proceedings of the Sixth Michigan State University Conference on Northeast Africa*, compiled by John T. Hinnant and Beth Finne (East Lansing: Michigan State University, 1992), 220.
4 See e.g. Abbas H. Gnamo, *Conquest and Resistance in the Ethiopian Empire, 1880–1974: The Case of Arsi Oromo* (Leiden: Brill, 2014).
5 Mordechai Abir, "The Emergence and Consolidation of the Monarchies of Enarea and Jimma in the First Half of the Nineteenth Century," *Journal of African History*, 6: 2 (1980), 205–219; Charles T. Beke, "On the Countries South of Abyssinia," *Journal of the Royal Geographical Society of London*, 13 (1843), 254–269.
6 See e.g. Jon Abbink, "An Historical-Anthropological Approach to Islam in Ethiopia: Issues of Identity and Politics," *Journal of African Cultural Studies*, 11: 2 (1998), 109–124; and Terje Østebø, "The Question of Becoming: Islamic Reform Movements in Contemporary Ethiopia," *Journal of Religion in Africa*, 38: 4 (2008), 416–446.
7 For more on this period, see two different though excellent monographs Bahru Zewde, *Pioneers of Change in Ethiopia: The Reformist Intellectuals of the Early Twentieth Century* (Oxford: James Currey, 2002), and Hanna Rubinkowska, *Ethiopia on the Verge of Modernity: The Transfer of Power During Zewditu's Reign 1916–1930* (Warsaw: Wydawnictwo AGADE, 2010).

8 Giampaolo Calchi Novati, "Colonialism as State-Maker in the History of the Horn of Africa: A Reassessment," in: *Proceedings of the 16th International Conference of Ethiopian Studies*, ed. by Svein Ege, Harald Aspen, Birhanu Teferra, and Shiferaw Bekele (Trondheim: NTNU, 2009), 234.

9 Numerous books and articles have been dedicated to the battle of Adowa, among those, see e.g. Paulos Milkias and Getachew Metaferia (ed.), *The Battle of Adowa: Reflections on Ethiopia's Historic Victory Against European Colonialism* (New York: Algora Publishing, 2005).

10 Aric Putnam, "Ethiopia Is Now: J.A. Rogers and the Rhetoric of Black Anticolonialism During the Great Depression," *Rhetoric and Public Affairs*, 10: 3 (2007), 420.

11 Assafa Jalata, *Contending Nationalisms of Oromia and Ethiopia: Struggling for Statehood, Sovereignty, and Multinational Democracy* (Binghamton: Global Academic Publishing, 2010), 21.

12 Walter Chichele Plowden, *Travels in Abyssinia and the Galla Country* (London: Longman, Green, and Co., 1868), 28.

13 Richard A. Caulk, "Armies as Predators: Soldiers and Peasants in Ethiopia, ca. 1850–1935," *International Journal of African Historical Studies*, 11: 3 (1978), 457–493.

14 Compare, for instance, Richard Pankhurst, *The Ethiopian Borderlands: Essays in Regional History From Ancient Times to the End of the 18th Century* (Lawrenceville and Asmara: The Red Sea Press, 1997), and Gadaa Melbaa, *Oromia: An Introduction* (Khartoum, 1988). Both deal with Ethiopian past but from distinctly different positions and perspectives.

15 Daniel Ayana, "The 'Galla' That Never Was: Its Origin and Reformulation in a Hinterland of Comparative Disadvantage," *Journal of Oromo Studies*, 17: 1 (2010), 1–40.

16 A very good analysis of these processes has been done by Tekeste Negash, *The Crisis of Ethiopian Education* (Uppsala: Uppsala University, 1990).

17 Tony Chafer, *The End of Empire in French West Africa: France's Successful Decolonization?* (Oxford: Oxford University Press, 2002), 119–120.

18 M. Asrat, *Modernity and Change in Ethiopia: 1941–1991: From Feudalism to Ethnic Federalism (A Fifty Years of Political and Historical Portrait of Ethiopia). A Participant-Observer Perspective.* Ph.D. Thesis (Troy, 2003), 21.

19 Some of these questions are raised by Baz Lecocq, *Disputed Desert: Decolonisation, Competing Nationalisms, and Tuareg Rebellions in Northern Mali* (Leiden: Brill, 2010), 1–3, and Klaas van Walraven, *The Yearning for Relief: A History of the Sawaba Movement in Niger* (Leiden: Brill, 2013), 3–38.

20 Ed Simone, "The Amhara Military Expeditions Against the Shawa Galla (1800–1850): A Reappraisal," in: *Proceedings of the First United States Conference on Ethiopian Studies, 1973* (East Lansing: Michigan State University, 1973), 138.

21 See e.g. Antonio Cecchi, *Da Zeila alle Frontiere del Caffa* (Roma: Ermanno Loescher and Co., 1886), 267–269.

22 See e.g. Tsega Etefa, *Integration and Peace in East Africa: A History of the Oromo Nation* (New York: Palgrave Macmillan, 2012).

23 Peter W. T. Baxter, Jan Hultin, and Alessandro Triulzi (eds.), *Being and Becoming Oromo: Historical and Anthropological Enquiries* (Uppsala: Nordiska Afrikainstitutet, 1996).

24 See e.g. Günther Schlee, "Redrawing the Map of the Horn: The Politics of Difference," *Africa*, 73: 3 (2003), 343–368.

25 Crawford Young, "Nation, Ethnicity, and Citizenship: Dilemmas of Democracy and Civil Order in Africa," in: *Making Nations, Creating Strangers: States and Citizenship in Africa*, ed. by Sarah Dorman, Daniel Hammett, and Paul Nugent (Leiden: Brill, 2007), 242.
26 Asafa Jalata, "Being in and Out of Africa: The Impact of Duality of Ethiopianism," *Journal of Black Studies*, 40: 2 (2009), 196.
27 Lahra Smith, *Making Citizens in Africa: Ethnicity, Gender, and National Identity in Ethiopia* (Cambridge: Cambridge University Press, 2014), 161.
28 See e.g. Jon Abbink, "Religion in Public Spaces: Emerging Muslim-Christian Polemics in Ethiopia," *African Affairs*, 110: 439 (2011), 253–274.
29 Tegegne Teka, "Amhara Ethnicity in the Making," in: *Ethnicity and the State in Eastern Africa*, ed. by M. A. Mohamed Salih and John Markakis (Uppsala: Nordiska Afrikainstitutet, 1998), 121.
30 Paulos Chanie, "The Rise of Politicized Ethnicity Among the Oromo in Ethiopia," in: *Ethnicity and the State in Eastern Africa*, ed. by M. A. Mohamed Salih and John Markakis (Uppsala: Nordiska Afrikainstitutet, 1998), 95.

2 The great imperial game in the Horn of Africa and its impact on current political processes in Somalia

Kateřina Rudincová

Introduction

At the end of the nineteenth century, Somali-inhabited territories were partitioned between the colonial powers, Great Britain, Italy, France, and Ethiopia. However, these colonies in the Horn of Africa had never been perceived as crucial by all the colonialist countries because of the physical conditions in Somali-inhabited territories which are to a large extent desert or semidesert areas and are not useable for agriculture but are usable for a pastoral way of living. Therefore, Somali-inhabited areas were important and were used by all these colonial powers because of the strategic reasons and their geographic position in the Horn of Africa in particular. As a consequence of the colonial partition, distinct political and territorial units with different forms of administration, economic, and social systems were formed. Even though Somali-inhabited areas have since been decolonized, the impact of colonialism in the Horn of Africa is still evident. The colonial powers delimited boundaries in the region regardless the ethnic, social, and economic structure of local societies, which later became the source of conflict, irredentist efforts, and the rise of Somali nationalism in particular, which itself was later to become the main ideology of General Siad Barre's regime. The same boundaries were an important factor in justifying the disintegration processes and the creation of independent Somaliland after the outbreak of the civil war. Colonial systems and their consequences may therefore be seen as the causes of the future instability of the Somali state.[1]

The main argument that underpins this chapter is that the colonial partition of Somali-inhabited areas, as well as the creation of distinct forms of colonial administration, had a great impact on the political processes in the current Somalia. Each colonial power utilized different mechanisms to govern its own territories and, therefore, each former colonial territory inherited a different political system, as well as political traditions. For example, the British used traditional clan elders for the administration of their protectorate. Their continuing importance is noticeable from the fact that elders played an important role in the conflict resolution processes in Somaliland in the early 1990s. The peace process in Somaliland exhibits the characteristics of the traditional or bottom-up approach to peace-building, which is claimed to be more successful in comparison to international efforts at conflict management.[2] The traditional peace resolution processes in the Somali context comprise the customary social conduct, the *xeer*, and the Islamic moral code; assemblies of elders, the *guurti*, used for conflict management; the role of elders as mediators; the *shirs* or clan councils as the arena for discussions; and *diya* payments or blood compensation.[3] In contrast to Somaliland, where the bottom-up approach to peace management has been used, in southern Somalia, the factional leaders were empowered as a consequence of the internationally-led peace resolution process.

The main aim of this chapter is to analyze the relations between colonial administrative systems, with a special focus on the British and Italian colonies, as well as the current political developments in Somalia. The first part of this chapter deals with the partition of Somali-inhabited territories during the "great imperial game" in the Horn of Africa in the nineteenth century. Following this, the sub-chapters are dedicated to an analysis of the impact of colonial administrations on the political, economic, and social systems. The concluding parts analyze the current political developments in Somali territories, on the basis of the colonial heritage. Special focus is given to the issue of boundary delimitation and the emergence of Somaliland, as well as to a comparison between the peace resolution processes in Somaliland and southern Somalia.

The partition of Somali-speaking territories during the great imperial game in the Horn of Africa

Political developments in the Horn of Africa during the nineteenth century were influenced by the rivalry between the great powers in relation to the division of the Somali territory. The most important political players of that time were Great Britain, Italy, France, and also, after the 1890s, the Ethiopian emperor, Menelik II. Great Britain, which established its military presence in Aden in 1839, was primarily motivated by a desire to enhance the quality of life of their Aden staff. Somalia was an area with a highly developed cattle breeding industry at that time, and therefore this was the particular focus of the British.[4] Another very strong motivation was the opening of the Suez Canal in 1869, as well as British efforts to control the maritime routes to India.

Egypt succeeded in occupying the coastal towns of Zeila and Berbera and even reached the city of Harar in eastern Ethiopia in 1875. Its efforts to penetrate into the Red Sea were motivated by a desire to control the headwaters of the Nile River, one of which was located in Ethiopia, and this ambition was supported by Great Britain. However, in 1885, Egypt was forced to withdraw from its positions because it was faced by the Mahdist revolt in Sudan. Britain, which replaced Egypt in northern Somalia, had been concluding agreements with local Somali clans[5] since 1881 and also with other colonial powers regarding the delimitation of boundaries in the region.[6] In 1887 the British protectorate of Somaliland was established.[7] In 1905, northern Somalia was transformed into a British colony. Besides possessions in the northern Somalia, Great Britain established also the Protectorate British East Africa, which incorporated present-day Kenya, including the area known as Jubaland, which was inhabited by ethnic Somalis.

Another player in the great imperial game in the Horn of Africa in the late nineteenth century was France, the great rival of Great Britain in the region. Its interests were not only economic, which can be demonstrated by the establishment of the Ethiopian-French business company in 1881, but also strategic. France had acquired colonies in Indochina and Madagascar and therefore needed a naval base on the African coast. The boundaries of the French colony in the Horn of Africa were defined by the Anglo-French treaty of 1888, and its territory included the present-day state of Djibouti.[8]

The presence of Italy in today's Somalia dates back to the late 1880s, when it gained the ports on the Benadir coast in southern Somalia. Italian trading companies such as Filonardi started to conclude agreements on the protection of the Somali clans on the Indian Ocean coast at that time. Great Britain supported Italian imperial efforts in the area of present-day Eritrea in order to prevent the expansion of Ethiopia under the rule of King Menelik. Bringing the Ethiopian territories under its administration was therefore the main motive of the Italian expansion in the region of the Horn. In 1885, Italy acquired the harbor of Masawa on the Red Sea coast, replacing Egypt in this area. Subsequently, it purchased additional ports on the Somali coast and expanded inland. In 1905, Italy introduced direct administration in its colonies, *Somalia Italiana*. In addition to regional geopolitical motives, the Italian expansion in the Horn was motivated by a desire to possess its own colonies, to establish a market for its goods, and to secure fertile areas where the government could settle poor Italian farmers.[9]

Another power that participated in the division of the Somali-inhabited territories was Ethiopia, under the leadership of Emperor Menelik II. It proved to be an important regional political player for the first time in 1887, when it recaptured Harar and subsequently defeated Italy in the battle of Adwa in 1896.[10] The Ethiopian position was then confirmed by the conclusion of the treaty with Great Britain, by which it gained Ogaden in the west of Somalia. This agreement later became the source of the Ethiopian-Somali border dispute.[11]

Traditional elites and clan leaders: differences between two colonial systems

The British administered their Protectorate of Somaliland through recourse to indirect rule,[12] which means that they used traditional local authorities in order to limit the resistance to colonialism. Therefore, the British incorporated elder leaders of the *diya*-paying groups into their administrative system and gave them the title of "chief" (*caaqil*). Chiefs had limited judicial power and were made responsible for the collection of certain taxes. Some of the clan elders participated in the judiciary within the local courts. In addition to the application of traditional and Islamic law, which was allowed to continue in the colonies, there was also the introduction of European colonial law. It led to the marginalization of traditional clan and religious authorities and to the empowerment of the *caaqils*, which resulted in resistance from the traditional clan leaders, the *sultaans*.[13] However, one of the legacies of indirect rule in northern Somalia was the preservation of indigenous political institutions, which were later to become the foundations of the post-conflict resolution process in Somaliland. The impact of the British indirect colonial rule in Jubaland may be seen also in the empowerment of local clan chiefs, coming from Marehan and Aulihan clans (from the Daarood clan family). For example, the clan leader Abdurrahman Mursaal from Aulihan clan even claimed the territory between Serenli and Wajir in 1915, however, was later defeated by the British colonial troops.[14]

In contrast, the Italian colonial administration in southern Somalia was highly centralized, with all the important positions being held by the officials dispatched directly from the colonial center. In the early stages, before the advent of fascist rule in 1923, the Italian colony was partly managed by the private Filonardi and Benadir trading companies. The centralization of the administration was accompanied by the suppression of local traditional institutions, which is recognized as being one of the causes of anarchy in southern Somalia in recent decades.[15]

According to Abdullah Mohamoud, the colonial administration in Somalia had a significant effect on the conflicts between the clans in three aspects: it used the disputes between the clans to consolidate its power; the very existence of the colonial administration caused conflicts between the clans, with the colonial administration using loyal groups to suppress resistance; and the war with the Dervish movement resulted in the rise of militarism in the region.[16] Charles Geschekter claims that "colonial traditions further accentuated regional distinctions" since the colonial regimes "exploited tensions among these groups to enhance their own power; existing differences were sharpened by the uneven impact of social and economic change."[17] Colonial administrations prioritized the clans which were willing to collaborate and which were better positioned because of their pre-colonial social arrangements. During the Trusteeship period, from 1950 to 1960, the Italian administration promoted the nomadic clans from the Majertin and Mudug regions despite the fact that these clans constituted minority groups in southern Somalia. Therefore, the Italians disrupted the natural division of power in their administered territory, which led to a struggle for power between particular clans.[18]

Colonial systems also had a significant impact on the economic situation in the region, since the boundaries of the colonies were established across clan territories, traditional pastures, and commercial zones of Somali clans. However, due to the fact that the colonial administration was not able to control the country effectively, nomadic migration continued almost unchanged.[19] The main exports from British Somaliland were cattle and related commodities, with the port of Berbera in northern Somalia playing an important role in the trade. Italian Somaliland was supposed to serve as a source of feedstock for the colonial country, and therefore local production was influenced by Italian demands. Huge banana plantations were established around the rivers Juba and Shabelle, and sugar, salt, and cotton were other commodities exported from the colony. The fascist government introduced monopolies in Somalia, and therefore it excluded the local community from participating in the trade.[20]

The creation of boundaries in the Horn of Africa and its consequences

One of the consequences of colonial administration in the Somali-inhabited territories is also the delimitation of boundaries, which resulted from the outcome of the Battle of Adwa in 1896. In the following years, the colonial powers in the region, France, Italy, and Great Britain, concluded several agreements with Ethiopia on border demarcation. A treaty between France and Ethiopia was signed in 1897, and this subsequently laid the foundations for the establishment of French Somaliland. Originally, Ethiopian territory was transferred to France under the condition that in the case of its withdrawal, it would be returned to Ethiopia. On the basis of the Ethiopian-British settlement, the area of Haud was ceded to Ethiopia in 1897. A treaty between Italy and Ethiopia on border demarcation was signed in 1908. However, the border was not finally demarcated, which caused a further crisis in 1935, the so-called Walwal incident.[21] Besides agreements concluded between Ethiopia and colonial powers, there were also several treaties on border demarcation concluded between particular European countries. For example, the border between British East Africa and Italian Somaliland was based on the Anglo-Italian protocol of 1891, which established the border between spheres of Britain and Italy on the river Juba.[22] However, in 1925, the originally British territory of Jubaland, which lies to the south of the river Juba, was ceded to Italy under the terms of the Article VIII of the London treaty, according to which if France and Britain gained new territories in Africa, Italy should be compensated by equitable possessions.[23] Therefore on the basis of the treaty, Italy was entitled to receive Jubaland as a compensation for its help during the World War I.[24] The southern part of Jubaland, however, remained as a part of the British possession in the Horn of Africa and later became known as Northern Frontier District (NFD). After its cession to Italy, Jubaland was first administered as a separate Italian colony Trans-Juba (Oltre Giuba), and one year later in 1926 incorporated into the Italian Somaliland. Therefore, in general, the colonial ambitions of the powers caused the division of the Somali-inhabited territories into five parts: French Somaliland (Djibouti), British Somaliland, Italian Somaliland, the Ogaden area of Ethiopia, and the territory of modern-day Kenya that is inhabited by ethnic Somalis, the so-called Northern Frontier District (NFD), which was under the administration of Great Britain during the colonial era.

In 1936, Italy united Italian Somalia with the eastern part of Ethiopia becoming a province of Italian East Africa and, subsequently, Italy invaded British Somaliland. With the changes in the geopolitical situation in the region in 1941, when all Somali territories, with the exception of French Somaliland, came under the administration of Great Britain, both the administration and the armed forces in southern Somalia became "Somalized."[25] First, the Somali political organizations created in the 1940s, such as the Somali Youth League and the Somali National League, made the territorial unification of Somali-inhabited territories their primary goal. Somali nationalists claimed that only a unified Somali state had the capacity to restore Somali unity and resist foreign oppression.[26] After World War II, the former entity of Italian Somalia was placed under the trusteeship system and, in accordance with General Assembly resolution no. 289 adopted in 1949, it was administered by Italy. In 1960, both British and Italian Somaliland gained independence and formed a united Somali Republic.[27] The commitment to the pan-Somali ideology adopted by the newly united Somalia was symbolized, for example, by the adoption of a new Somali flag, representing all five Somali-inhabited areas, with the future aim being to incorporate them in a unified state.

One of the causes of state collapse in Somalia was the irredentist aspiration to unite all Somali-inhabited territories into one state, which culminated in the war over Ogaden between Somalia and Ethiopia in 1977–1978. The subsequent huge influx of refugees from Ethiopian Ogaden into Somalia caused conflicts over grazing lands between the incoming Ogadeni clans and native Isaaqs. As a consequence of this war, the hopes of achieving a

Greater Somalia were shattered, pan-Somalist ideology was abandoned, and the first opposition movements against the Barre regime, such as the Somali Democratic Salvation Front (SSDF) were established.[28]

Currently, the creation of colonial borders serves as one of the legitimization strategies of Somaliland, which in accordance with the principle of the inviolability of colonial borders stresses the former independence of British Somaliland before the merger of two colonial units, the British and the Italian, into a single unitary state.[29] The British Somaliland gained its independence even five days earlier than the Italian Trusteeship and, moreover, this five-day independence of British Somaliland in 1950 was recognized by 35 states of international community including all five permanent members of the UN Security Council.[30] The constitution of Somaliland defines the territory of this de-facto state as follows: "The territory of the Republic of Somaliland covers the same area as that of the former Somaliland Protectorate."[31] The territory of Somaliland is thus based on the boundaries of the former British Somaliland, which was established in 1887, and its borders were delimited on the basis of international agreements concluded between 1888 and 1897.[32]

A contrast between the traditional peace management process in Somaliland and the internationally led peace initiatives in Somalia

After the creation of a unified Somali state, it became obvious that the state-building process would be extremely difficult since the former British and Italian Somalia had experienced different historical, social, and economic development pathways during the colonial era. New and lethal conflicts over the share of power between the northern and southern clans emerged and reached a climax during the violent regime of General Siad Barre, who came to power in the coup of 1969. Barre effectively manipulated clan affiliations and social class differences. His politics resulted in the break out of civil war, firstly in northern Somalia in the 1980s and later developing into full-scale violence and Barre's removal from power in 1991. Subsequently, Somalia fell into anarchy, with individual armed factions all striving to gain a share of power.[33]

The inconclusive security and political situation in Somalia led various organizations, including the UN, to make efforts to mediate a peace. However, the peace process in northern and southern Somalia differed significantly. Ken Menkhaus developed the typology of reconciliation processes in Somalia between 1991 and 1995, and he has concluded that the national-level, faction-based, and UNOSOM-sponsored conferences were the least successful aspects of reconciliation efforts since they did not include traditional elders and were based on negotiations between armed factions.[34] The UN-sponsored conferences in southern Somalia ignored the affected communities and instead empowered the military factional leaders, such as general Aideed. They were held mostly in neighboring countries and influenced by the interests of host countries. Moreover, signed agreements often had a short life-span.[35]

In Somaliland, the grassroots peace resolution process achieved more sustainable results. Traditional conflict management processes have generally included traditional Somali social groups, such as *diya*-paying groups, institutions such as the *shir*, or assembly, and clan elders in particular. The crucial part of the conflict resolution mechanisms has been Somali customary law, the *xeer*. In Somaliland, institutions based on traditional social systems were established with the leading role played by the elders and this is considered to be a heritage of the British indirect rule approach. Therefore, according to Jhazbhay, "revisiting the comparative British and Italian colonial legacies along Somali coast provides some perspective on the foundations for post-conflict reconciliation."[36]

The current political system of Somaliland is the result of various clan peace conferences held since 1991, when Siad Barre was ousted from power. The independence of Somaliland was declared at the Grand Conference of the Northern Peoples in Burco on 18 May 1991. Even though its independence was not recognized by any state from the international community, the state-building process followed. The Borama conference, held in 1993, adopted the National Charter, which formalized the principles of traditional peace resolution and proposed a hybrid system of government based on modern as well as traditional Somali institutions, the so-called *beel* system.[37] The legislature comprises the Parliament, which consists of the House of Representatives (the Lower chamber) and the House of Elders (the *Guurti*, the Upper chamber). The formalization of Somaliland's institutions ended with the election of Haji Mohamed Egal as the first president of independent state. At the Hargeysa Peace and Reconciliation Conference of the Somaliland clans, held in 1996, the "democratization" process was inaugurated and subsequently this was followed by the referendum on the Somaliland constitution and the first democratic presidential elections in 2001 and 2003 respectively.[38]

According to Menkhaus,[39] the strength of traditional communities in Northern Somalia may be perceived, in addition to the contribution made by the colonial heritage, as resulting from two other factors: the isolation of the North from the socioeconomic processes taking place in southern Somalia; and the greater ethnic homogeneity of the North.[40] Therefore, the value of the traditional conflict management mechanisms should not be perceived as universal but rather as situational. Yet, it is undeniable that peace management based on traditional leaders in Somaliland proved to be more fruitful than internationally led peace-building efforts in Somalia, which is still in the midst of turmoil resulting from the civil war.

Moreover, the political identity of Somaliland, which has been created from below, is shaped by the colonial past of this territory as a British protectorate. Great Britain is continually seen as the "patron" who is possibly able to help Somaliland achieve international recognition, and in this context there is a clear emphasis on its colonial past under the rule of British law.[41] In general, Great Britain is perceived as being the most influential supporter of independence in Somaliland when compared with other European countries. Analogically, Italy as a former colonial power was directly involved in the peace process and in the development of the humanitarian intervention, operation "Ibis," in southern Somalia, and this was achieved despite the opposition of the warring parties and the United States because of their ongoing support for Siad Barre's regime.[42]

Conclusion

Even though Somali-inhabited territories were decolonized decades ago, the legacies of colonial systems are still evident. One of them is the demarcation of boundaries which divided the Somali population into five distinct colonial states. This division resulted in the rise of nationalist ideas during the era of decolonization and in the efforts to reunify all parts into a single unified Somali state. However, with the collapse of the Somali state in the 1990s, the irredentist claims were abandoned and more particularistic ideas spread among the Somalis, resulting in the declaration of independence of Somaliland within the area of the former British Somaliland. It is the distinct colonial history five-day independence recognized by 35 states of international community as well as the delimited colonial boundaries, which are the most important arguments used by Somaliland political representatives to justify their claims for international recognition.

Besides the delimitation of boundaries, the colonial administrations had an enormous impact on the social and political systems, because they empowered elders, as in the case of British Somaliland, or they suppressed their power, as in Italian Somalia. The legacy of colonial systems in Somalia has been evident during the reconciliation process that began after the outbreak of the Somali civil war. On the one hand, the peace process in Somaliland was secured by the incorporation of traditional clan leaders, who formed the Upper House of the Parliament, the *Guurti*, and on the other hand, the peace-resolution process in southern Somalia empowered the military leaders and, to some extent, it excluded the elders and civil society. Even though the conditions and traditions of both parts of Somalia are different, the success of the traditionally based peace management process in Somaliland is undeniable. Therefore, actors and mediators of peace resolution processes in southern Somalia might possibly be inspired by the peace process in Somaliland and seek to engage civil society and its traditional leaders in the peace-management activities within their country.

Notes

1 Brons, Maria, *Society, Security, Sovereignty and the State in Somalia: From Statelessness to Statelessness?* (Utrecht: International Books, 2001), 129; Abdulahi A. Osman, "Cultural Diversity and the Somali Conflict: Myth or Reality?" *African Journal on Conflict Resolution*, 7: 2 (2007), 93–134.
2 I. William Zartman (ed.), *Traditional Cures for Modern Conflicts: African Conflict "Medicine"* (London: Lynne Rienner Publishers, 2000).
3 Oliver Ramsbotham and Tom Woodhouse, *Peacekeeping and Conflict Resolution* (Routledge: London, 2013), 160.
4 Abdullah A. Mohamoud, *State Collapse and Post-Conflict Development in Africa: The Case of Somalia (1960–2001)* (West Lafayette, IN: Purdue University Press, 2006), 66.
5 By the end of 1884, an agreement on friendship and trade between Great Britain and the clans of Cise, Gadabuursi, Habar Garhajis, Habar Awal, and Habar Tol Jalo was signed. They maintained the independence of the clan territories and were not perceived to be protectorate treaties; therefore, there was no legalization of any colonial occupation of Somali territory. Anthony J. Carroll and B. Rajagopal, "The Case for the Independent Statehood of Somaliland," *American University Journal of International Law and Policy*, 8: 2/3 (1993), 657–658.
6 In 1888, the Anglo-French agreement, and subsequently the Anglo-Italian treaty in 1894, and the Anglo-Ethiopian agreement in 1897, were concluded. Benjamin R. Farley, "Calling a State a State: Somaliland and International Recognition," *Emory International Law Review*, 24: 2 (2010), 779; Mark Bradbury, *Becoming Somaliland* (London: Progressio, 2008), 26.
7 Saadia Touval, *Somali Nationalism: International Politics and the Drive for Unity in the Horn of Africa* (Cambridge, MA: Harvard University Press, 1963), 37; Maria Brons, *Society, Security, Sovereignty and the State in Somalia: From Statelessness to Statelessness?* (Utrecht: International Books, 2001), 130–132.
8 Ioan M. Lewis, *A Modern History of the Somali: Nation and State in the Horn of Africa* (New York: Ohio University Press, 2003), 49; Abdullah A. Mohamoud, *State Collapse and Post-Conflict Development in Africa: The Case of Somalia (1960–2001)* (West Lafayette, IN: Purdue University Press, 2006), 66.
9 Abdullah A. Mohamoud, *State Collapse and Post-Conflict Development in Africa: The Case of Somalia (1960–2001)* (West Lafayette, IN: Purdue University Press, 2006), 67; Maria Brons, *Society, Security, Sovereignty and the State in Somalia: From Statelessness to Statelessness?* (Utrecht: International Books, 2001), 133–134; Ioan M. Lewis, *A Modern History of the Somali: Nation and State in the Horn of Africa* (New York: Ohio University Press, 2003), 50–56.
10 In 1889, Italy entered into the agreement of Wichale (Ucciali) with the then Ethiopian king, Menelik. After the death of Emperor Yohannis, Menelik became

the new Ethiopian Emperor and began to consolidate his power. Italians, however, demanded the establishment of the protectorate over Ethiopia in the 1890s and their claims then led to armed conflict between the Italian and Ethiopian armies at Adwa. Maria Brons, *Society, Security, Sovereignty and the State in Somalia: From Statelessness to Statelessness?* (Utrecht: International Books, 2001), 133–134.

11 Margaret Castagno, *Historical Dictionary of Somalia* (Metuchen, NJ: The Scarecrow Press, 1975), 10.

12 See e.g. Mahmood Mamdani, "Historicizing Power and Responses to Power: Indirect Rule and Its Reform," *Social Research*, 66: 3 (1999), 859–886.

13 Mark Bradbury, *Becoming Somaliland* (London: Progressio, 2008), 28; Ioan M. Lewis, *A Pastoral Democracy: A Study of Pastoralism and Politics Among the Northern Somali of the Horn of Africa* (Oxford: Oxford University Press, 1961), 200–201.

14 Saadia Touval, *Somali Nationalism: International Politics and the Drive for Unity in the Horn of Africa* (Cambridge, MA: Harvard University Press, 1963), 66–67.

15 Mark Bradbury, *Becoming Somaliland* (London: Progressio, 2008), 29.

16 Abdullah A. Mohamoud, *State Collapse and Post-Conflict Development in Africa: The Case of Somalia (1960–2001)* (West Lafayette, IN: Purdue University Press, 2006), 60–61. For a history of Dervish movement, see e.g. Ioan M. Lewis, *A Modern History of the Somali: Nation and State in the Horn of Africa* (Athens: Ohio University Press, 2003), 63–91.

17 Charles Geschekter, "The Death of Somalia in Historical Perspective," in: *Mending Rips in the Sky: Options for Somali Communities in the 21st Century*, ed. by Hussein M. Adan and Richard Ford (Trenton, NJ: The Red Sea Press, 1997), 70–71.

18 Abdulahi A. Osman, "Cultural Diversity and the Somali Conflict: Myth or Reality?" *African Journal on Conflict Resolution*, 7: 2 (2007), 102.

19 Maria Brons, *Society, Security, Sovereignty and the State in Somalia: From Statelessness to Statelessness?* (Utrecht: International Books, 2001), 145–146.

20 Ioan M. Lewis, *Making and Breaking States in Africa: The Somali Experience* (Trenton, NJ: The Red Sea Press, 2010), 10–16.

21 The Walwal incident erupted as a result of the delimitation of the border between Ethiopia and Italian Somaliland. Although the Walwal area belonged to Ethiopia as a result of the Battle of Adwa, Italy claimed it because significant water resources were to be found there. The diplomatic dispute escalated into armed conflict and the Ethiopian Emperor submitted the dispute to the League of Nations, which, however, proved to be ineffective. Great Britain and France essentially sacrificed Ethiopia and the situation resulted in the Italian occupation of the country in 1936, along with the creation of Italian East Africa (*Africa Orientale Italiana*); Maria Brons, *Society, Security, Sovereignty and the State in Somalia: From Statelessness to Statelessness?* (Utrecht: International Books, 2001), 135–136; Bahru Zewde, *A History of Modern Ethiopia, 1855–1991* (Athens: Ohio University Press, 2001), 153.

22 Saadia Touval, *Somali Nationalism: International Politics and the Drive for Unity in the Horn of Africa* (Cambridge, MA: Harvard University Press, 1963), 46.

23 C. J. Lowe and F. Marzari, *Italian Foreign Policy, 1870–1940* (London: Routledge, 2001), 187.

24 James H. Burgwyn, *Italian Foreign Policy in the Interwar Period, 1918–1940* (Westport: Praeger Publishers, 1997), 21–22.

25 Maria Brons, *Society, Security, Sovereignty and the State in Somalia: From Statelessness to Statelessness?* (Utrecht: International Books, 2011), 150–151.

26 Charles Geschekter, "The Death of Somalia in Historical Perspective," in: *Mending Rips in the Sky: Options for Somali Communities in the 21st Century,* ed. by Hussein M. Adan and Richard Ford (Trenton, NJ: The Red Sea Press, 1997), 71.

27 Abdulahi A. Osman, "Cultural Diversity and the Somali Conflict: Myth or Reality?" *African Journal on Conflict Resolution,* 7: 2 (2007), 101–102.

28 Charles Geschekter, "The Death of Somalia in Historical Perspective," in: *Mending Rips in the Sky: Options for Somali Communities in the 21st Century,* ed. by Hussein M. Adan and Richard Ford (Trenton, NJ: The Red Sea Press, 1997), 75.

29 Mark Bradbury, Adan Yusuf Abokor, and Haroon Ahmed Yusuf, "Somaliland: Choosing Politics Over Violence," *Review of African Political Economy,* 30: 97 (2003), 457; Anthony J. Carroll and B. Rajagopal, "The Case for the Independent Statehood of Somaliland," *American University Journal of International Law and Policy,* 8: 2/3 (1993), 662.

30 Peter Roethke, "The Right to Secede Under International Law: The Case of Somaliland," *Journal of International Service,* 20: 2 (2011), 36.

31 Constitution of the Republic of Somaliland (2001). Available online: www. somalilandlaw.com (accessed 20.8.2014).

32 Mark Bradbury, Adan Yusuf Abokor, and Haroon Ahmed Yusuf, "Somaliland: Choosing Politics Over Violence," *Review of African Political Economy,* 30: 97 (2003), 457.

33 See e.g. Florence Ssereo, "Clanpolitics, Clan-Democracy and Conflict Regulation in Africa: The Experience of Somalia," *Global Review of Ethnopolitics,* 2: 3–4 (2003), 25–40.

34 Ken Menkhaus, "International Peacebuilding and the Dynamics of Local and National Reconciliation in Somalia," in: *Learning From Somalia: The Lessons of Armed Humanitarian Intervention,* ed. by Walter Clarke and Jeffrey Herbst (Boulder: Westview Press, 1997), 42–63; Iqbal Jhazbhay, *Somaliland: An African Struggle for Nationhood and International Recognition* (Institute for Global Dialogue and South African Institute of International Affairs, 2009), 41.

35 Ismail I. Ahmed and Reginald Herbold Green, "The Heritage of War and State Collapse in Somalia and Somaliland: Local-level Effects, External Interventions and Reconstruction," *Third World Quarterly,* 20: 1 (1999), 124.

36 Iqbal Jhazbhay, *Somaliland: An African Struggle for Nationhood and International Recognition* (Institute for Global Dialogue and South African Institute of International Affairs, 2009), 28.

37 See e.g. Mark Bradbury, *Becoming Somaliland* (London: Progressio, 2008); Maria Brons, *Society, Security, Sovereignty and the State in Somalia: From Statelessness to Statelessness?* (Utrecht: International Books, 2001).

38 For the democratization process, see e.g. Mark Bradbury, Adan Yusuf Abokor, and Haroon Ahmed Yusuf, "Somaliland: Choosing Politics Over Violence," *Review of African Political Economy,* 30: 97 (2003), 455–478.

39 Ken Menkhaus, "Traditional Conflict Management in Contemporary Somalia," in: *Traditional Cures for Modern Conflicts: African Conflict "Medicine,"* ed. by I. William Zartman (London: Lynne Rienner Publishers, 2000), 189.

40 The northern Somali population comprises the Dir, Isaaq, and Darod clans.
41 Marcus V. Höhne, "Political Identity, Emerging State Structures and Conflict in Northern Somalia," *Journal of Modern African Studies*, 44: 3 (2006), 403.
42 Paolo Tripodi, *The Colonial Legacy in Somalia: Rome and Mogadishu: From Colonial Administration to Operation Restore Hope* (New York: Palgrave Macmillan, 1999), 143–145.

3   Small but strategic

Foreign interests, railway, and colonialism in Djibouti

Jan Dvořáček and Jan Záhořík

Introduction

For decades, the Horn of Africa has attracted the attention of world powers, especially for its strategic position on the geopolitical map that enabled
to control the important space in the Middle East and in the Indian Ocean.
Since the opening of the Suez canal, the whole region became one of the
most important sites of sea waterways connecting European, African, and
Asian trade. French colonial activities in the Horn started in this period
and culminated with the construction of a strategic railway Djibouti-Addis
Ababa. All above-mentioned aspects played very significant role in decolonization time. Belated independence of the sea port Djibouti caused tensions
in French-Ethiopian relations that were extremely complicated after the
independence of Somalia whose territorial claims had intensified in 1960.
The chapter deals with specific position of small French territory which
became the last continental colony in Sub-Saharan Africa. The main focus
will be concentrated on economic, political, and ethnic environment of Djibouti in the time of high geopolitical tensions in Africa.

Djibouti is one of the smallest states in Africa in an area of Bab-al-Mandeb
Strait which belongs to very strategic territories connecting Africa with the
Middle East. Despite its small size, Djibouti is relatively ethnically heterogeneous being from its colonial beginnings composed of Afars, Somalis,
and Arabs.[1] The size and ethnic composition of Djibouti also shows one
significant aspect of the Horn of Africa in general which is its extreme diversity and multiple colonial legacies including Italian, French, British as well
as a unique case of independent Ethiopia, itself being blamed of colonizing
various peoples on the edge of the Ethiopian Highlands. Geographically,
Djibouti is set in one of the most inhospitable and hottest climates on Earth.
However, it is so strategic that it benefits from presence of French and US
military bases.[2] Djibouti's history from colonial times until nowadays has
been influenced by constant rivalry between major ethnic groups, Afars, and

Issas which affects cross-border tensions in neighboring Ethiopia.[3] Until Djibouti's independence, France supported local Afars while the first Djiboutian president in 1977 reflected a significant change, being an Issa, and establishing a single-party system.[4]

From an economical point of view, the most significant aspect of Djibouti's existence has been the railway connection with Ethiopia and thus the trade in the larger Horn of Africa, and sea routes in the Indian Ocean and the Middle East.[5] Djibouti thus plays a role of a "border territory" which connects Africa with the Arab Peninsula and overseas trade, and at the same time it served as the main, though isolated, French territory in East Africa dominated by the British. Not surprisingly, already before the creation of Djibouti, its territory, and ports, such as Obock, served as crucial places for transfer of goods, ammunition, and weaponry for the Ethiopian military forces, such as those of Menelik.[6] This trend only increased until the battle of Adowa in 1896 and even after,[7] primarily due to the Addis Ababa-Djibouti railway. This chapter deals with foreign (primarily French and Ethiopian) interests and strategic position as well as economic importance of Djibouti, related mainly to the railway connecting the port with the Ethiopian interior.

The railway Djibouti-Addis Ababa

The decision to construct a railway connecting Ethiopia's interior with the Red Sea and Indian Ocean was of crucial importance in the process of economic development of Ethiopia as well as presence of European powers inside Ethiopia. From the very beginning of its existence, the railway Djibouti-Addis Ababa represented an economic backbone not only for Ethiopian Empire, but also for the whole region of the Horn of Africa. Its construction started in the time of great territorial expansion of the Emperor Menelik II, which was at the same time followed by a systematic advancement of some colonial powers such as Italy, France, and Great Britain. A history of this railway illustrates clearly the rise and fall of the Empire in last decades of its existence. Symbolically, a sad destiny of this railway also reflects last decades of Ethiopian contemporary history and its political and social turbulences.

A great part of employees of the railway Djibouti-Addis Ababa had been still using French as a lingua franca even after the withdrawal of French colonial administration from Djibouti. This railway was the first and, for a long time, the most important industrial project in Ethiopia: it was the shortest traffic connection between the heart of Ethiopia and the Red Sea with a length of 784 km and altitude rising from the sea level in Djibouti to 2 400 meters above sea level in Addis Ababa.[8]

The project of its construction was clearly marked by attempts of colonial powers to dominate the Horn of Africa. Having dedicated his life to the development of the empire, Menelik II was well aware that Ethiopia during centuries without access to the sea, would stay isolated in Africa. The desire to have an access to the sea led him to develop a plan for building up infrastructure that would allow connecting to Djibouti, French maritime port of the first rank.

But access occurred only after the resounding victory of Adwa in 1896, after which the French authorities agreed the free passage of the railroad through the Côte Française des Somalis/French Somaliland (CFS). The authorization of the railway in Ethiopia caused more problems on the French territory. First, there was a real concern of European progressing colonization. On the other hand, the owners of camel caravans feared the competition that would threaten their business activities.

After a few projects developed by several engineers, the final concession was given to architect of the new Ethiopian capital Addis Ababa, Swiss engineer Alfred Ilg.[9] The operating company, whose name was " Compagnie impériale de chemins de fer éthiopiens" (CIE), had begun to build the railway in 1897. This company was created by Ilg and French engineer, Léon Chefneux.

At the beginning, this company had some financial complications, and administrators appealed to British for a financial support. In 1902, the company was placed under control of the colonial authorities, and the railway influenced the foundation of a new city, Dire Dawa. The Tripartite Agreement of 13 December 1906 divided Ethiopia into zones of influence of France, Italy, and the United Kingdom.[10]

In 1908, the CIE gave its name to the "Compagnie du chemin de fer franco-éthiopien," French S.A. corporation.[11] From 1909 to 1959 the CFE was chaired by Charles Michel Côte. During his long presidency, the line from Djibouti to Addis Ababa was officially opened May 9, 1917, after 20 years of hard work and some financial obstacles. After World War II, investments allowed to reduce considerably a travel time. In 1948, the CFE was providing direct connection between Djibouti and Addis Ababa by a tri-weekly passenger service stopping at Dire Dawa, Awash, and Modjo in 23 hours, as well as a direct service for transportation of the goods.[12]

The structure of the CFE had been considerably changed by an agreement dated 12 November 1959 between France and Ethiopia. On the basis of this agreement, the capital of the Company was divided equally between French and Ethiopian shareholders, and the Board of Directors was composed of six Ethiopian and six French members. Large sums were spent on renewal, modernization, and expansion of its facilities and its equipment.

As such, from 1960 until June 1966, the Company invested 19 million francs in the complete reconstruction of stations Dire Dawa and Addis Ababa. The Ethiopian action in this area was greatly facilitated by obtaining grants from the French government which made it possible to organize intensive trainings in France (SNCF in particular) each year in order to form qualified staff of the railway. This treaty bestowed Ethiopia facilities in the port of Djibouti, as well as in the traffic by rail.[13]

The project of construction of Sidamo railway was also deeply discussed in the 1960s but it has been never carried out despite an agreement from 1964 that ensured its implementation. On 27 June 1977, the French Territory of the Afars and Issas gained its independence and took a new official name the Republic of Djibouti. In March 1981, Compagnie du chemin de fer Djibouto-Éthiopienne (CDE) was founded and its management was entrusted to the Joint Executive Board.

Djibouti at the center of French-Ethiopian interests

Djibouti was already at the end of the nineteenth century a place of frequent diplomatic meetings especially in regard to worsened Ethio-Italian relations after the Adowa battle and due to Russian presence in the Horn of Africa as one of the supporters of the Ethiopian (Orthodox) state.[14] For the French, connection between Djibouti and Addis Ababa had also one more important meaning, and that was Dire Dawa, the main station of the route, which served as kind of a "sanatorium for the French community in Djibouti, who migrated in large numbers during summer to avoid the torrid climate of their colony."[15]

At that time, area of Djibouti reached 23 000 km², populated by about 800 000 inhabitants. The territory hosted American, French, and German military units, as well as a minority of Japanese soldiers. Their presence proved a high strategic importance in the Eastern Africa and the position of the first order on one of the most frequented sea routes. The territory of today Djibouti has been attracted by its neighbors and maritime powers through its whole existence. It was the last African continental territory, under which France exercised its sovereignty.[16]

What was the main reason for the French foreign affairs to control this territory until 1977? In order to properly analyze this considerable delay, if compared to other former French colonial possessions, we have to go back to the era that preceded the conquest of Africa. As mentioned in many books on colonization, the Scramble for Africa between European powers officially began at the Berlin conference (1884–1885), despite of the fact that the main actors of colonial rule were firmly established in Africa long before this conference.

This was also the case of the French presence in the territory of which the coast extends into the Gulf of Tadjoura, in broader perspective part of the Gulf of Aden. In close proximity of this strategic region is situated the

Bab el-Mandeb Strait, which separates the Republic of Djibouti and Yemen linking the Red Sea to the Gulf of Aden and the Indian Ocean.

Relations between France and Ethiopia have a long tradition. In the seventeenth century, an adventurer from Montpellier called Verneuil, exercised in Ethiopia two important functions: premier minister and generalissimo. In 1699, Dr. Poncet cured King Yassou I of leprosy, and afterwards became his adviser. Bonaparte thought to introduce Abyssinia into a vast system of Oriental policy. In 1843, Louis-Philippe concluded with the king of Shoa an alliance that remained as the charter of the Franco-Abyssinian friendship.

This policy of collaboration was accomplished by Léonce Lagarde's mission that tied relationships with the authorities of Harar and engaged discussions that should lead to the sending of a diplomatic mission in Addis Ababa in 1896. Menelik II welcomed Lagarde warmly by giving him a hug in front of all his court. The Emperor expressed his wish to renew the treaty concluded by Louis-Philippe that embodied the role of Djibouti as the only official outlet for Ethiopian trade. The treaty also assured to France many important privileges. Lagarde, unlike some other agents of European colonialism in Africa, triumphed without spending money and without bloodshed.

The Negus let Lagarde put on his royal robe with gold embroidery and named him Duke. Ras Makonnen gave him a rare proof of his confidence and friendship. When leaving for the battle of Adwa, he laid into the arms of Lagarde a cradle with a sleeping child and said: " I entrust to you my son. If I die in the war, swear me that you will bring him up " The child he held was the future Emperor of Abyssinia, Haile Selassie.[17] In 1897, Ethiopia and France signed a treaty that delineated borders between Ethiopia and the new French colonial possession. Until 1930s, the French had to negotiate the borders in the region with the colonial powers of Italy and Great Britain and focused on further geographical exploration of its territory.[18]

A few years later, when the London Conference was held (1906), the three colonial powers (England, Italy, and France) guaranteed the integrity of Abyssinian territory, not without flirting with the idea of sharing some territorial gains in case some disturbances occurred. Following these negotiations, Ethiopia began to distrust the French friendship. From that time, the Abyssinian Empire was threatened, as the Eritrean coast was coveted by Italy, sources of Nils by England, and territory of Tadjoura Gulf by France.[19]

Between French Somaliland and Ethiopia, there existed common interests due to their proximity. From the beginning of the French presence in the Horn of Africa, the two regional powers (France and Ethiopia) followed a common policy, which was motivated essentially by the aim to establish trade relations.

After the liberation of Ethiopia in 1941, it was already clear that repossession of Franco-Ethiopian railway, as well as the development of the port of

Djibouti, would be the primary interest of France. However, the existence of a strong British influence led France to negotiate directly with the British military administration a provisional arrangement with the aim to replace French agents on the railroad. The British military control was explained by the maintenance of territory in Somalia and the desire to control the outlet on the Red Sea.[20]

After the World War II, Djibouti was transformed into a free port; and the administration and the police were provided by the French authorities. Ethiopia disposed of special stores, where goods could be subject of commercial manipulation from the side of Ethiopian customs.[21]

In 1953, at the time of the "Gaullist opposition," General de Gaulle made a big trip around the French Union. He decided to visit all the territories of West and Equatorial Africa, the islands of the Indian Ocean and Djibouti. At the end of this long journey, he made a visit to the Emperor Haile Selassie. It should be added that General de Gaulle very much appreciated Haile Selassie, whom he had known in London. Both were leaders during the war and their fight within national resistance gave them a reputation of national heroes. Despite the mutual respect that existed between these two figures, the first visit was marked by an ignorance of diplomatic protocol.[22] The state visit in August 1966 was important for several reasons. First, de Gaulle returned to Haile Selassie the official visit that the Emperor had made in 1959 (along with one visit that he had taken in 1963 for private purposes). It took place in the background of the critical situation in Djibouti, where a series of demonstrations for the independence culminated during the visit of General de Gaulle in 26 August 1966.

The question of Greater Somalia was largely discussed during the first meeting. This issue began an "*ever green*" of Franco-Ethiopian talks since Haile Selassie's visit to Paris in 1959. The Ethiopian government was concerned not only about Soviet arms shipments to Somalia, which accumulated in 1966, but also about the Arab world that would encircle Ethiopia after a planned withdrawal of the British from Aden (1968). Haile Selassie sought to equip his army relying on French military cooperation in order to create a balance as the American supplies were considered insufficient and ineffective to tackle Somali equipment.

De Gaulle doubted the potential threat of the Somali Republic and promised to review Haile Selassie's requirements. At the end of the interview, the Ethiopian Prime Minister Aklilou Habte Wold, turned the page by evoking the Ethiopian concerns about the CFS:

> But we must also consider the fact that Djibouti was part of the Ethiopian Empire. More than ever, since the railway linked Djibouti to Addis Ababa, Djibouti has been our natural outlet . . . If local authorities

respect the rights of the majority Afar, the interests of Ethiopia will be saved. If France leaves, we would not like to be disadvantaged, we would not like that the Issas have everything and the Afars nothing.[23]

The French attitude toward the possession was discussed during each meeting of high political representatives. To avoid repeating still the same, it is sufficient to note that in France there was no question of accepting the claims of Djibouti's independence even if the rest of continental Francophone Africa had been already independent. Confronting critical voices, France evoked the referendum of 1958, and, being well aware that public opinion in the CFS gradually changed during the 1960s, she used the presidential elections of 1964 as an asset of its irreversible hegemony.

On the other hand, the issue of Ethiopian pressure towards strengthening claims on independence of Djibouti should be emphasized. At this point, we can refer to diplomatic sources reporting time of Menelik II and his project of "Great Ethiopia." It is the evocation of an old treaty between Léonce Lagarde and Ras Makonnen (father of Haile Selassie) which had defined the terms of the French commitment to Djibouti. First, Ethiopian officials expected a response to the potential arms trade. General de Gaulle said very directly: "In principle, France had no intention of the military strengthening of Ethiopia." This response was so persuasive that the Ethiopians did not dare to continue in negotiations. It should be added that the Ethiopians expected the negative response and the failure of the negotiations was not uncommon for a country whose business strategy at that time was to increase loans with low interest rates that were proposed by some socialist countries.

East Africa met a crucial period with the referendum in CFS organized by the French administration following the troubles in Djibouti. The distribution of "yes" and "no" corresponded almost exactly to the proportion between the Afars who voted yes, and Issas who voted no.[24] The above-mentioned referendum proposed to the people a new statute granting the territorial autonomy, while remaining within the French Republic. The referendum in March 1967 reconstituted ties with France under a new denomination – Territory of the Afars and Issas (TAFI) – which therefore represented the population instead of possession.[25] It was a success for the Afars, and the former vice president Ali Aref Bourhan[26] could then run of office in the Assembly again. Thus TAFI gained widened autonomy with the new government dominated by a party Afar – National Union for Independence (UNI).

The UN was highly critical of the polling for the referendum because France did not accept the presence of UN observers, even though it was a common practice that the UN missions were allowed to monitor votes in the Third-World countries. This refusal to cooperate with the United Nations, and an obscured political atmosphere that was characterized by numerous irregularities around the poll, had very significant impact on relations between France and its last colonial possession in Sub-Saharan Africa:

> It was sad that France had done so much for the cause of decolonization, has tarnished its image in the eyes of the world. It was clear that the people of French Somaliland wanted independence. On the other hand, it must be noted that there was a real threat of cessation of economic aid if the people of French Somaliland should have voted for independence.[27]

French official diplomatic sources described the referendum from March 1967 as democratic, noting that the population of Djibouti did not vote for independence. According to statistics, 39 031 voters participated in referendum, from those 22 523 voted for remaining with France and 14 734 for independence.[28] Somali government did not accept the result, considering that the referendum was not performed in a democratic way. France strongly opposed pan-Somali movement based on an idea of creation of "Greater Somalia" and thus including Djibouti.[29] So did Ethiopia, with a significant Somali minority in Ogaden region. Regional and ethnic rivalries and existence of political parties with different backing (Somalian, Ethiopian) led to an increase of violence in the 1970s shortly before the Djiboutian independence was proclaimed.[30] However, in order to secure its post-colonial policy and dominance in its former colonies, France made defense agreements with various different African nations, which allowed Paris to keep military bases in Africa, including Djibouti.[31]

Conclusion

Despite its small size, Djibouti has always been an important place that divided and connected the Horn of Africa. Surrounded by Italian, British, and Ethiopian empires, French territory that later became Djibouti contributed to further separation of Somali-speaking peoples but also connected Horn of Africa's interior with international trade by railway and port. However, shortly after the fall of colonial rule in Djibouti and an imperial regime in Ethiopia, the railway connection ceased to exist and only recently began to experience a modest revival. The economic and political situation of Djibouti became dramatic after revolutionary changes in neighboring Somalia and Ethiopia when both long-time dictators were overthrown after prolonged wars. Government in Djibouti lost its supporters so that refugees and demobilized soldiers had to be employed in order to fight against armed groups.[32] However, not long after, in 1998, the economic importance of Djibouti increased almost overnight due to the

Eritrean-Ethiopian war and its significance resembled the early colonial era of Addis Ababa-Djibouti railway fame. This led directly to expansion and upgrade of port in Djibouti in order to fulfill the needs and demands of Ethiopia's international trade.[33] Ethiopia remains the primary international client for the port in Djibouti. However, this does not mean that relations between both countries are calm as shown by some recent examples of quarrels over the level of taxation and costs. On the other hand, a tangible benefit coming from good relations with Ethiopia can be seen in electricity, now exported from Ethiopia, which has led to significant decrease of prices and has helped economy in Djibouti to grow.

Notes

1 See e.g. Alain Rouaud, "Pour une histoire des Arabes de Djibouti, 1896–1977," *Cahiers d'études africaines*, 37: 146 (1997), 324.
2 Jennifer N. Brass, "Djibouti's Unusual Resource Course," *Journal of Modern African Studies*, 46: 4 (2008), 525.
3 Yasin Mohammed Yasin, "Trans-Border Political Alliance in the Horn of Africa: The Case of the Afar-Issa Conflict," in: *Borders and Borderlands as Resources in the Horn of Africa*, ed. by Dereje Feyissa and Markus Virgil Hoehne (Oxford: James Currey, 2010), 88–89.
4 Peter J. Schraeder, "Ethnic Politics in Djibouti: From 'Eye of the Hurricane' to 'Boiling Cauldron'," *African Affairs*, 92: 367 (1993), 206–207.
5 For instance, Djibouti port is vital for the khat trade connecting Ethiopia with other countries: see Ezekiel Gebissa, *Leaf of Allah: Khat and Agricultural Transformation in Harerghe, Ethiopia (1875–1991)* (Oxford: James Currey, 2004).
6 Sven Rubenson, *The Survival of Ethiopian Independence* (Addis Ababa: Kuraz Publishing Agency, 1991), 369.
7 See e.g. Richard Caulk, *"Between the Jaws of Hyenas": A Diplomatic History of Ethiopia (1876–1896)* (Wiesbaden: Harrassowitz, 2002), 603–605.
8 Rosanna Van Gelder Pineda de, *Le Chemin de fer de Djibouti à Addis-Abeba* [Railway From Djibouti to Addis-Abeba] (Paris: L'Harmattan, 1995); Vincent Basuyau, *Le chemin de fer de Djibouti à Addis Abeba*. Mémoire de DEA (Université de Paris I-Panthéon-Sorbonne, 1991); Alain Gascon, "Fin du chemin de fer, fin de Grande Éthiopie. La mort annoncée du chemin de fer de Menilek," in: *Le chemin de fer en Afrique*, ed. by J.-L. Chaléard, C. Chanson-Jabeur and C. Béranger (Paris: Karthala, 2006), 35–54.
9 Heribert Küng, *Staatsminister Alfred Ilg (1854–1916), ein Thurgauer am Hof Kaiser Menelik II. von Äthiopien*. Thesis-Verl. (Zürich, 1999), *Alfred Ilg – Der weiße Abessinier*, un film de Christoph Kühn (Suisse, 2003).
10 Bahru Zewde, *A History of Modern Ethiopia, 1885–1991* (Oxford: James Currey, 2001), 84–85.
11 Prijac (Lukian), *Antony Klobukowski et le traité franco-éthiopien de 1908* (Paris: Aresæ, 2003).
12 CADN (Centre des Archives diplomatiques de Nantes), AA-Ambassade/B, carton 29, Bulletin of Franco-Ethiopian Chamber of Commerce, n° 4, May 1948.
13 CADN, AA-Ambassade/B, carton 60, Speech of the Emperor Haile Selassie during the official visit of General de Gaulle in Ethiopia, 28 August 1966.

14 David Levering Lewis, *The Race to Fashoda: European Colonialism and African Resistance in the Scramble for Africa* (New York: Weidenfeld and Nicholson, 1987), 123–125.

15 Bahru Zewde, "The City Centre: A Shifting Concept in the History of Addis Ababa," in: *Society, State, and History: Selected Essays*, ed. by Bahru Zewde (Addis Ababa: Addis Ababa University Press, 2008), 485.

16 In CADN we can find a dozen of archival funds focusing on French-Ethiopian Railway (Addis-Ababa – Djibouti). For instance, the fund *Afrique 1918–1940*: *K – Afrique 1918–1940 – Éthiopie, Industrie – Travaux publics (Travaux publics – Transport)*, cartons 40–49.

17 CADN, AA-Ambassade/B, carton 20, *Extrait de l'Auvergne chez elle et à travers le monde par Raymond Cortat*, 5.

18 Simon Imbert-Vier, *Traces des frontières à Djibouti. Des territoires et des hommes aux XIXe et XXe siècles* (Paris: Karthala, 2011), 145–147.

19 Ibid.

20 CADN, AA-Ambassade/B, carton 20, Franco-Ethiopian talks on Djibouti 1944–1948, Memorandum on the French policy in Ethiopia on 22 June 1944, GB/TP, 1–3.

21 CADN, AA-Ambassade/B, carton 20, About the Port of Djibouti: Letter of the Minister of Foreign Affairs to Ambassador of France in Addis Abeba, A. L. n° 29, 7 December 1945.

22 Philippe Gaillard, *Foccart parle I: entretiens avec Philippe Gaillard* (Paris: Fayard, 1995), 105–106.

23 Ibid., 528.

24 *Année africaine 1967*, Chronique des États – le Territoire des Afars et des Issas, 515.

25 From July 1967, the territory was renamed and became *Territoire des Affars et des Issas* (TFAI).

26 AREF (Bourhan Ali) – Vice-President of the Government Council from 1960 to 1966, President of the Council from 1966 to 1967.

27 CADN, AA-Ambassade/B, carton 21, Telegram of the IV. Committee to diplomatic body in Paris – Territoire français des Afars et des Issas, n° 4271, New York, 15 December 1967, signed by M. Armand Bérard.

28 *Documents diplomatiques français* (DDF) *1967*, t. I, 334. From a total number of 39 312 registered voters, there were 37 221 votes cast, of which 22 555 for keeping tights with France and 14 666 for independence. It is very to judge the conduct of this referendum, but the results published in official documents in France expressed more or less ethnic decomposition between Afars and Issas. On the other hand, there is no evidence that Issas voted freely, as mentioned in the quoted volume of DDF.

29 Thomas A. Marks, "Djibouti: France's Strategic Toehold in Africa," *African Affairs*, 73: 290 (1974), 101.

30 New Trouble for French Colony on Red Sea, *MERIP Reports*, 45 (1976), 22.

31 Thomas A. Marks, "Djibouti: France's Strategic Toehold in Africa," *African Affairs*, 73: 290 (1974), 95–97.

32 Abdo A. Abdallah, "State Building, Independence and Post-Conflict Reconstruction in Djibouti," in: *Post-Conflict Peace-Building in the Horn of Africa*, ed. by Ulf Johansson Dahre (Lund: Lund University, 2008), 275–276.

33 David Styan, *Djibouti: Challenging Influence in the Horn's Strategic Hub.* Chatham House Briefing Paper, AFP BP 2013/01, 5.

4   A small piece of Africa

Creating the British colony of the Gambia

Filip Strych

Introduction

Only a small number of African countries were immune from colonization. No matter how long the period of colonization, it has undoubtedly
left its mark, either for good or ill. The golden time of colonialism is associated with the early 1880s, when the so-called Scramble for Africa took
place between the main European colonial powers such as Great Britain and
France, closely followed by Italy, Germany, Belgium, and the two former
great imperial powers of Spain and Portugal. Once these colonial empires
had been dismantled, the process having started in the mid-twentieth century
and concluding in the early 1990s, (i.e. Namibia, de facto in 1990; Eritrea,
de facto in 1991, de iure in 1993), the discussion in relation to the colonial
legacy was unleashed. Various issues from the ethnic, religious, and socio-
economic spheres – old ones as well as new ones – are now addressed within
the context of modern African studies and its branches such as history, social
anthropology, ethnography, and even modern archaeology. A good example
of this relates to how the abolition of the slave trade affected the local economies of the nineteenth century. On the one hand, nobody denies that the
original slave trade caused suffering and pain to thousands and thousands
of lives and disrupted small societies and kingdoms all around Africa. On
the other hand, some believe that the abolition of the slave trade also caused
difficulties for some of the local rulers. Changes in the economic system
caused many kingdoms to fall because the trade of new commodities such
as beeswax, groundnuts, and gum did not fill the financial gap created by the
abolition of the slave trade. These kingdoms depended on the slave trade.
Changes in trade patterns were one of the biggest phenomena in relation to
the economic history of West Africa.[1] Many scholars have been interested in the
main areas of the British colonization in West Africa like the Gold Coast,
the Niger Delta. However, the British also left their mark in the small region
around the River Gambia.

This chapter explores how such the transition took place on the West Coast of Africa, particularly in the Gambia area. Even though the aforementioned region is relatively small, it played a significant role in the British colonial history in the wake of the nineteenth century. The Gambia once again became one of the British places of interest. European slave traders considered the Gambia, Upper Guinea, and the Gold Coast as the main slaving areas in the West Africa.

Growing levels of European trade changed the old trading system in the area of Upper Guinea. Once the slave trade was abolished, "legitimate" trade in such commodities as peanuts, timber, coffee, and rubber reduced the need for long-distance transport as plantations were established nearer to the ports and stations. The peanut industry quickly became the most important component of trade on the Upper Guinea Coast, and its yields caused a revolution in the economy of the communities living along the river banks.[2] The first half of the nineteenth century witnessed a number of important events that changed all aspects of life in Senegambia. The Congress of Vienna, held in 1814, signaled the restoration of British and French power in Senegambia after their eclipse during the Imperial Wars. This recovery took place at the same time as the gradual transition from commercial mercantilism to industrial capitalism was under way. This shift was important for the whole of Europe because it helped to establish new types of supremacy over the pre-capitalist economies in West Africa. After the British abolished the slave trade, Senegambia became a source of raw materials for Europe. It became both a center of agriculture production as well as a market for European industrial goods. These changes occurred in the midst of the economic crisis that was caused by the abolition of slavery. The old colonial empires wanted to secure their spheres of influence and hold fast because they were afraid of new powers such as the United States. The Southern Rivers region, with its many estuaries, provided a very good location for the continuance of an illegal slave trade.[3] In this chapter, I will discuss the creation of the small British colony of the Gambia. However, since there are already several significant monographs[4] that focus on the Gambia, I plan to summarize what has already been written about the country, supplementing this with official reports from the National Archives in Kew, London. The outcome will be an overview of the early history of the British settlement on the River Gambia.

Early settlement

Although the Gambia represents only a small part of Africa,[5] its history includes many shifts, twists, and turns relating to slavery, various types of trade – especially the slave trade and the trade in groundnuts – and last, but not least, in the field of warfare. The first Europeans came to the Gambia from Portugal and Italy, Luiz de Cadamosto and Antoniotti Usodimare respectively, and they dropped anchor in the river-mouth in 1455. It was not until 1661 that the first British outpost on the River Gambia was established on James Island, approximately 25 miles from the river's mouth. The British were only to abandon this station 118 years later, in 1779, because it had ceased to serve its original purposes. At the beginning of the nineteenth century, Earl Bathurst, who was strongly opposed to the slave trade, set out to develop a "legitimate" trade environment. One of the ways he identified as necessary for achieving his ultimate goal was to gain control of the River Gambia and its estuary. The best possible solution was to establish a base at the mouth of the river. Thus, Sir Charles MacCarthy (the Governor of Sierra Leone) sent Captain Alexander Grant to build a new fort there. In April 1816, an expedition from Gorée under Captain Alexander Grant headed towards Banjul Island and renamed it as St. Mary's Island. Alexander Grant then established a settlement named Bathurst, which was in honor of Sir Earl Bathurst, the then Secretary of State for the Colonies. Grant proceeded to construct army barracks for a maximum of 80 soldiers and mounted several cannons to guard the estuary of the Gambia River. However, this task was more than difficult to fulfill because of Bathurst's location. The island itself lies on flat land that is regularly flooded.[6]

In 1818, the total population of the new settlement was around 600. By 1826, this figure had risen to 1,800 (excluding the garrison), of which 30 were Europeans. In the 1830s, a ship laden with liberated African refugees landed in Bathurst and the Liberated African Yard became a new home for those "repatriated" Africans. The Colonial Government then built Goderich Village near Oyster Creek, specifically to assist these Liberated Africans. By the middle of the nineteenth century, the local population of Bathurst was 4,000 as well as their being 190 colonialists.[7] Most of them were British, but a few French had settled there as well.

Theoretically, the new settlement remained the dual responsibility of Parliament and the Company of Merchants until 1821, when an Act of Parliament stripped the Company of all its rights in the Gambia, as well as on the Gold Coast.[8] In 1822, Sir Charles MacCarthy, after his tour of West Africa, commented that the improvements in commerce in Bathurst were greater than in any of the other posts occupied by her Majesty's forces on the coast. After three months, and a lot of effort on the part of Grant's men, and having endured high death rates from malaria and other swamp fevers, the island became secure enough for it to be used as a trading stronghold, thus allowing British traders to transfer their base from Gorée Island to Bathurst.[9] Thus, the Gambia fell under colonial rule once again, along with James Island, St. Louis, and many other trading stations in Senegal, which together shaped the Province of Senegambia from 1765 to 1783. Nevertheless, the Gambia was not yet a Crown Colony. The Gambia and the Gold Coast fell under the jurisdiction of the governor-general of Sierra Leone. The commandant of the garrison and, after 1829, a lieutenant governor exercised local authority in the Gambia. However, this arrangement was not favored in Bathurst.[10] The British Government subsidized only the cost of defense. Apart from that, the customs duties on imports should have been the main source of income in the maintenance of the colony. In June 1843, the administrative relationship between Sierra Leone and the Gambia was terminated and this meant that the Gambia became an independent Crown Colony with its own governor, who was obligated to the secretary of state for the colonies. Independence only lasted for 23 years, i.e. until 1866, when the administration over the British West African settlements became centralized.[11] Despite claiming to be doing otherwise, the British expanded the area around the River Gambia on several occasions. After capturing Banjul, they bought MacCarthy Island in 1823, acquired the "Ceded Mile"[12] in 1826 and British Combo in 1840,[13] as well as receiving a trading post called Albreda as part of an exchange deal with France in 1857. The British added more areas in the 1880s.[14]

The foundation of Bathurst

Bathurst did not have officer quarters or any "building that could be properly called so." The British condemned the former officers' quarters in 1825 and later tore them down. A new building was found to be unsuitable for a physician (or an officer of his rank). Moreover, during the rainy season, three officers occupied one room and men soon became ill after living in such conditions for a period of time. Major Alex Findlay pointed out these concerns on numerous occasions in his reports. One might add that either he was dedicated to his men's welfare or that he was simply obliged to write such reports because his soldiers felt uncomfortable and were seriously dissatisfied with the conditions in the barracks. Moreover, living in such conditions made them sick and some of them actually died. Findlay defended himself with a statement that represented not only his own opinions but those of the physician and the medic: "Other Europeans were in their very best state of health with better accommodation during the rainy season. The conditions of sick men could not be attributed to anything but to their accommodation."[15]

As for the military hospital, it had a kitchen, a guardhouse, a mortuary, and a stable. Some other parts were in need of thorough repair. The original design for a hospital had envisaged space for 60 to 70 patients, a room for a medical officer, and a surgery. Major Findlay suggested separating the convalescents from the severely sick men, which was not possible in the single small barrack room that was available. It was planned that the soldiers' barracks would accommodate 150 men but one of the rooms was used as a hospital and the other was divided into officers' quarters. Men were crowded together to the extent that it was difficult to sleep. Other rooms on the ground floor served as a carpenter's shop and a canteen. Major Findlay found them largely unfit for habitation during the rainy season. Findlay proposed to build new barracks for his men. A further building served as a bake house, a cookhouse, and a blacksmith's forge. It was ill adapted for any of these purposes, being a close, low, and smoky place. Thus, he recommended clearing it out and using it as a commissariat store. He proposed building a comfortable barrack room on top of it. The bake house, cookhouse, and the blacksmith's forge would be better suited along the wall. Findlay claimed that he had to paint these wooden constructions every year otherwise they would fall down. Sir Charles MacCarthy built a convalescent hospital for the sum of 900 pounds, situated 10 miles south of the town of Bathurst. Like all other buildings in the station, this was only painted once. Expenses increased because of these repairs.[16]

One of the more important buildings in Bathurst was the Government House. It was a well-constructed stone building, surrounded by a wall, which enclosed a kitchen, a guardhouse, stable, and a small garden. Major Findlay wrote "It costs a quat sum of money, in consequence of being blown down by a severe tornado, when it was ready for put the roof on." However, the building was not finished. The insufficient funds prevented that. Findlay further reported,

> the house hadn't glass windows and when tornado came, the whole house had to be shut up which made him as dark as prison. The external woodwork was completely destroyed because it was not regularly painted before. Major Campbell's orders turned this house into officers' barracks by which means the furniture was damaged as well as many other parts of the buildings (doors, verandas etc.). It needed a great repair.[17]

To sum up, Findlay was in need of a new Government House as well as a new officers' barracks (which he mentions earlier in the report).

One of the major issues with St. Mary's Island was the water level. Because of this, the hospital, Government House, the officers' quarters, and the battery, when built, were placed between 46 and 55 meters back from the high water mark. In the 1820s, the spring tides came up the steps of Government House and quickly undermined the battery. Major Findlay came up with "the cheapest and best plan," which consisted of driving piles into the ground in front of these buildings and layering a quantity of brushwood between them, along with loose stones. He believed that this would serve to collect sand and cause a bank to be thrown up along the beach. Because the whole of St. Mary's Island was frequently prone to flooding, the British built a cleaning and drainage system on the island, which was no longer maintained by the time of Findlay's arrival. As he stated, "Nothing was done. All the drains around the island were filled up. If they are cleaned and have the proper attention, no water can lodge on St. Mary's Island. This can be done by a hard labor by men committed to do it with a supervisor." It is clear that failure to maintain the systems would result in significant damage being experienced by the settlement in general. Findlay definitely made a sound proposal for ensuring that the natural swampy state of the land was addressed (in the same way as the ground had been improved around Fort Campbell on MacCarthy Island).[18]

Finally, but of great importance, the most essential elements of the settlement were the defenses. The main defense installation was an open battery, on which three guns could be mounted. However, one of them had been removed to Fort Bullen. The two remaining ones were beyond repair and needed to be replaced. In Findlay's words: "They were so rotten that a second shot from them would knock them to pieces, so that we shall require a new carriages." The government office knew how important it was to secure the safety of the river-mouth; it was clear that another battery on Barra Point would be sufficient to protect the settlement. Findlay also advocated the installation of a blockhouse or battery, which could protect the town from the rear. Findlay was aware of the danger of an attack on the landward side. It would have been easy to land on the extreme point of the island and march into the town with little opposition.[19]

Regional trade and entrepreneurs

After the establishment of the British settlement in Bathurst, a small but influential European community established itself. These pioneers were mainly British merchants who had arrived from Gorée, which had returned to the French rule in 1817. Many of the Europeans in the colony at any time were British but a number of French entrepreneurs lived there as well.[20] Most of the merchants had small family businesses. In addition, there was also an import and export business, Forster and Smith, which supplied goods on credit to individual customers in the West African market.[21]

The British merchants at Gorée operated in affiliation with the military commandant in order to forge the policy of the station. Thus, they gladly acceded to Sir Charles MacCarthy's order to transfer judicial, legislative, and executive powers to the new settlement of Bathurst. MacCarthy established a Settlement Court, which was responsible for the maintenance of peace and the determination of welfare rights in the settlement, and also had additional responsibilities in relation to the collection of revenue and expenditure. Moreover, MacCarthy founded a formal judicial system in which, on the one hand, all minor civil cases fell under the Court of Police and Equity jurisdiction and, on the other hand, the Settlement Court heard appeals from the lower court as well as being responsible for criminal cases. Nevertheless, when the Gambia and the Gold Coast were formally placed under the authority of Sierra Leone in 1821, all local customs and regulations were repealed. In other words, most of the cases were dealt with by the Justice of the Peace based in Sierra Leone, who appeared in the Gambia only irregularly.[22]

The decision to transfer all the most important local authority offices from Bathurst to Freetown in 1821 made the merchants very uncomfortable and they disliked the decision intensely. This was mainly because in practical terms they lost control over their revenues and expenditures, as well as the fact that they were now subject to all government decisions. Their ultimate goal was to safely conduct trade along the River Gambia. For this reason, Alexander Grant purchased an island, which he named after Sir Charles MacCarthy, and then established a small garrison on it. As mentioned earlier, he also added the Ceded Mile, acquired from the King of Barra.[23]

However, the Colonial Office was strongly opposed to any expansion of the colony. Proposals by the merchants were often rejected by the Colonial Office. Major Alex Findlay was strongly opposed to the French. He was tasked with taking any action, including the use of force, to stop French vessels from their trading station in Albreda from illegally trading in contraband goods along the river. Findlay sought to address the numerous complaints made by merchants in Bathurst and he prohibited any French vessel from entering the river-mouth. These vessels were required to pay a tax before they could proceed up river. Nevertheless, this decision breached the Treaty of Paris and thus the secretary of state for the colonies banned it.[24] The main reason why the Colonial Office hesitated to extend the Colony was because of the potential for creating further liabilities associated with any additional expenditure. The Colonial Office also proved reluctant, especially after 1826, to sanction the annexation of further territory, as the merchants were demanding, because this might lead to unwanted commitments and expenditure. One particular treaty, signed by Governor Campbell of Sierra Leone in 1827, would have resulted in the annexation of land at Brikama, but this remained a dead letter; the secretary of state for the colonies repudiated another, which had been signed by the acting lieutenant governor, William Hutton, and the King of Wuli in 1829.[25]

Transition from illegal to legitimate trade

The British abolitionist stance during the Congress of Vienna in 1814 forced the leading European powers, along with the United States, to abolish the slave trade. There existed two parallel branches of trade in Senegambia. Long-tenured Euro-African slave-trading families such as the Ormond family and the Curtis family had been responsible for the first illegal slave trade. The latter, responsible for developing a legal commodities trade, were of interest to those British and French trading companies that were interested in conquering the Southern Rivers area. As a result of this, Southern Senegambia was in very good shape during the first half of the nineteenth century. On the other hand, Northern Senegambia experienced a very tough period. This was because of the plantation scheme experiment, which led into speculative gum trading from 1830 onwards. The peanut trade established very favorable circumstances that supported the expansion of French control over the region.[26]

Gorée, the Gambia. and Sierra Leone were the main settlements in the region. With the illegal slave trade in decline, the French established new plantations in Waalo and the Cape Verde peninsula. This represented the French response to the new situation; they were unable to continue with the slave trade so they were forced to seek out other business options. The French trading companies from Marseille and Bordeaux actively searched for new business opportunities. They had a preference for peanut oil as the main lubricant for the French industrial market. On the other hand, the British opted for palm oil. The French peanut industry began to grow. Firstly, they entered the Southern Rivers area and then they opened up plantations in Kajoor.

The Northern Senegambia was a very important business area during the nineteenth century. Britain started its anti-slavery ventures in Freetown, the main outpost of Sierra Leone.[27] However, the other leading powers of that period, such as the United States and France, were strictly against the abolition of slavery because they were still able to make large profits from this business. These countries were opposed to the boarding and searching of their vessels by British naval forces. In addition, the layout of the Southern Rivers, with its numerous river-mouths,[28] was ideal for black market transactions and the pursuit of the illegal slave trade.[29] It was impossible to control and monitor the whole area.[30]

After the capture of one of their slaving vessels, the Euro-Africans changed their approach and started to establish coffee plantations. These plantations served as a perfect cover for further slave trade activities. The Euro-Africans forced the captured slaves to work on their newly established plantations during the rainy season.[31] John Ormond, one of the most prolific slave traders, died in 1833. His death presaged the symbolic end of the era in which slave traders were completely integrated into local life through their marriages with the daughters of local aristocrats. Nevertheless, the Euro-African influence in the region lasted until the late 1840s, thanks to the parallel activities associated with the illegal slave trade and legitimate trade activities. It remains unclear as to how many slaves were sold during the nineteenth century. Thousands of slaves were shipped from the Southern Rivers region and slavery was not fully abandoned in the area immediately.

Conclusion

British colonial rule, aided in part by French colonial rule, was instrumental in establishing the origins of the colony of the Gambia. After the first British settlers arrived from Gorée (which was retaken by France at the end of 1810s), they started building a small settlement on St. Mary's Island. This new part of the British Empire received its name in honor of Sir Earl Bathurst, the Secretary of State for the Colonies. However, it was made clear that the Colonial Office in London had no plans for expanding the St. Mary's Island settlement; they simply wished to control the estuary of the river, and they were aware that any further expansion of the colony would require increased expenditure. Adopting a different position, the newly arrived merchants were strongly opposed to such plans and attempted to persuade the Colonial Office of the advantages associated with their plans for expansion. The merchants found a strong supporter in the person of Major Alex Findlay, who challenged the French trade in contraband along the river. Findlay proposed that a tax should be paid on every vessel entering the river. However, the Colonial Office rejected these proposals, although Findlay successfully acquired a number of areas, such as MacCarthy Island, Barra Point, and the Ceded Mile. Aside from the British and their plans, some other important events shaped the early days of the Gambia. For more than three centuries, the slave trade had represented the main source of income for the local rulers. At the beginning of the nineteenth century, the Slave Abolition Act caused, perhaps, the biggest change in the West African economy. Local kings and rulers had to find a new way of supplementing their reduced incomes. The legitimate trade in such commodities as beeswax and ivory was not sufficient. However, in the early 1820s, the French came up with the idea of planting peanuts, which has remained as the main crop in the area until today. As we have noted, the former British colony of the Gambia experienced various changes in the first half of the nineteenth century, before it finally became an independent crown colony in 1843.

Notes

1 Robin Law (ed.), *From Slave Trade to "Legitimate" Commerce: The Commercial Transition in Nineteenth-Century West Africa* (Cambridge: Cambridge University Press, 1995), 1–5. See also: Kenneth Swindell and Alieu Jeng, *Migrants, Credit and Climate: The Gambian Groundnut Trade, 1834–1934* (Leiden and Boston: Brill, 2006).

2 George Brooks, "Peanuts and Colonialism: Consequences of the Commercialization of Peanuts in West Africa, 1830–1870," *Journal of African History*, 16: 30 (1975).

3 Barry Boubacar, *Senegambia and the Atlantic Slave Trade* (Cambridge: Cambridge University Press, 1998), 129.

4 See Arnold Hughes and David Perfect, *A Political History of the Gambia* (Rochester: Rochester University Press) or John Milner Gray, *History of the Gambia* (London: Frank Class, 2006).

5 The total area of the country covers 10,689 square kilometres (4,007 square miles).

6 Alex Findlay to R. W. Hay, 5th April 1828, Colonial Office 87/1, the National Archives, Kew, London.

7 CO 87/1, the National Archives, London.

8 Arnold Hughes and David Perfect, *A Political History of the Gambia* (Rochester: Rochester University Press, 2006), 7.

9 Alex Findlay to R. W. Hay, 5th April 1828, Colonial Office 87/1, the National Archives, Kew, London.

10 Arnold Hughes and David Perfect, *A Political History of the Gambia* (Rochester: Rochester University Press, 2006), 7.

11 The settlements were the Gambia, the Gold Coast, Lagos, and Sierra Leone.

12 A land strip on the north side of the river bank; 1.6 kilometres /1 mile wide and 58 kilometres/36 miles long. It was extended in 1832.

13 Later called Kombo St. Mary, a 40 square kilometres, 25 square miles, large piece of land located west of Bathurst and extended in 1853.

14 Arnold Hughes and David Perfect, *A Political History of the Gambia* (Rochester: Rochester University Press, 2006), 7.

15 Alex Findlay to R. W. Hay, 5 April 1828, Colonial Office 87/1, the National Archives, Kew, London.

16 Ibid.

17 Ibid.

18 Ibid.

19 Ibid.

20 Arnold Hughes and David Perfect, *A Political History of the Gambia* (Rochester: Rochester University Press, 2006), 23.

21 Florence K. O. Mahoney, *Government and Opinion in the Gambia 1816–1901* (London: University of London, 1963), 39–42.

22 John Milner Gray, *History of the Gambia* (London: Frank Class, 1966), 323–324.

23 Arnold Hughes and David Perfect, *A Political History of the Gambia* (Rochester: Rochester University Press, 2006), 56.

24 John Milner Gray, *History of the Gambia* (London: Frank Class, 1966), 399–402.

25 Ibid., 339–342.

26 Barry Boubacar, *Senegambia and the Atlantic Slave Trade* (Cambridge: Cambridge University Press, 1998), 133.

27　A group of philanthropists founded Freetown in 1787.

28　The main rivers in this are the Rio Nunez, the Rio Pongo, and the Rio Cacheu.

29　Many slave-trading families maintained the slave trade until the middle of the nineteenth century. The most powerful players were John Ormond, John Holman, William Skelton, and Emmanuel Gomez. These well-educated Britons quickly adjusted themselves to the new economic situation in the whole of the Southern Rivers region. John Ormond owned between 5,000 and 6,000 slaves at the peak of his trading success.

30　Bruce Mouser, *Trade and Politics in the Nunez and Pongo Rivers 1790–1865* (Bloomington: Indiana University Press, 1971), 39.

31　In 1826, they planted almost 10,000 coffee bushes along the Rio Pongo.

5 The French protectorate in Tunisia

A visitor's insight

Jakub Kydlíček

Introduction

It can be clearly stated that The French protectorate in Tunisia (from 1881 onwards), as elsewhere, was clearly established and managed in response to the concept of "civilizing mission" ("mission civilisatrice") – the idea of spreading the culture of the empire by civilizing the native population and integrating the country into the French cultural sphere. The focus of this study is on how the civilizing mission concept was reflected in the practical steps taken by the protectorate administration. First of all, it is necessary to consider the question of how the French elites regarded the "objects to be civilized," i.e. what was their opinion of the indigenous population. The present study is a micro-historical inventory based on examples and illustrations preserved for us by travelers from that period (individuals who had varying degrees of affinity with the protectorate and ideas relating to the civilizing mission).

This chapter seeks to outline the main contours of the image of the local population as seen through the eyes of travelers from the late nineteenth century, and attempts to clarify the concept of ethnicity, as well as to identify the most common themes that emerge in the selected travelogues. The key items are the selected passages that explain the characteristics of various ethnic groups, along with their internal relationships and rivalries. To some degree, the attention of the writers was focused on ethnographic descriptions – especially the descriptions of the customs and homes of the "Indigenes." This study does not set out to provide a detailed analysis – the aim is to offer an inventory picture, thus providing the reader with an appropriate foundation for understanding the ideological context of the French protectorate.

Paradoxically, it is sometimes the case that "historically unreliable" sources can be identified as one of the means of providing us with knowledge as to the history of a country. In particular, travel diaries and personal notes can be seen as resources that do not fully satisfy the requirements of traditional historiographical methodology, either because of their content (it is often the case that they either misrepresent information or provide an amateurish interpretation of ethnographic data) or their degree of formality (the production of an accurate record was not necessarily the primary concern of the author of the diary) On the other hand, the diaries and travel records do provide us with a "mirror" in relation to the "big" history, as reflected in archival material from government records. The aim is primarily to provide a micro-historical spotlight on the individual items that appear in the inventory of the travelers' ethnographies. The terms of such a micro-historical approach will also emphasize the social dimension of the examined events, without trying to locate them within a macro-historical model.[1]

In addition, the geographical focus of the study corresponds with current micro-historical trends – thus drawing attention to the periphery (in this case, the largely insignificant and "rightly-forgotten" province of Arad). The limited range of the evidence base necessitates the application of an historical science approach when dealing with the "broad descriptions."[2]

The resource base for the present study is based on a selection of travelogues from the years 1882–1896: Henri Lorin's *Une Promenade en Tunisie* (1896),[3] Marius Bernard's *De Tunis à Tripoli* (1892),[4] and Chevalier Ernst de Hesse-Wartegg's *Tunis – The Land and the People* (1882).[5]

The authors, the context, and the expeditions

Henri Lorin's (1866–1932) *Promenade en Tunisie* (1896) is a travel diary that is completely in tune with the spirit and ideas associated with the civilizing mission concept. The purpose of this educational pamphlet is encapsulated in the following text: "almost fifteen years since France established itself in Tunis . . . to answer the questions that the fellow citizens of France are not able to answer." This "booklet" aims to dispel some of the doubts raised at the beginning of the occupation, and provide an *"impression d'ensemble"* that will present "detailed information" before the French audience (which means that the text was particularly persuasive in relation to identifying the usefulness of the protectorate itself). The author of the work, Henri Lorin (later a distinguished professor of history and geography in Bordeaux) was able to undertake his journey thanks to the efforts of the Régence Minister of the Protectorate government in Tunis, René Millet. Together with other "honorable men" and "specialists in different areas," Lorin embarks on a journey.[6] His journey around Gabès was undertaken between the 21st and 28th November 1896. Initially, Lorin took a short ride to the village of Chenini (near Gabes), then travelled on horseback to Hades, about 40 kilometers away.

Lorin had a direct experience with the daily life in the Protectorate and its reforms. He occupied a position at Lycée Carnot de Tunis, and as the distinguished figure, he witnessed the implementation of educational system as proposed by Louis Machuel and his political companion Bernard Roy.[7] The "Promenade en Tunisie" was his first official publication and could be seen as rather exceptional from his other writings of academic character.[8]

During his later years, Lorin was active not only as academician in the field of "colonial geography," but also as a writer and commissioned several articles in "colonial" magazines. One of those was "Le quinzaine colonial," which had been published on bi-weekly basis and was read by both French colonial personnel. His contemporaries, mostly theorists of colonization, mentioned him in their papers. One flagrant example is a study "utilization of military element in populating of Tunisia" (*L´Utilisation de l´élément militaire pour le peuplement de la Tunisie*).[9] In this article, Lorin is gloriously honored as "historian, educated in geography and doctor of philosophy" (*agrégé d´histoire et de géographie, docteur des lettres*). The nature of Lorin´s writings were not always scientifically serious, but rather popular accounts on actual events in the Protectorate. Example of such account is his "reportage" from the Port of Sfax, where he described a process of "industrialization" of the Tunisian land, which he saw as a tool of "civilizing" the indigenous people.[10]

Ernst von Hesse-Wartegg (1851–1918) worked in Tunisia for several months in 1881 and most of his commentary is thus based, according to him, on "eyewitness observations, supplemented by consular reports and communications with representatives of the Bey government" [sic]. The motivation behind the release of the travelogue was mostly educational – in the preface the author points out how little European readers are aware of this country, where "so much has happened." Unlike Lorin and Bernard, Hesse-Wartegg is more of an adventurer and writer than a promoter of the civilizing mission. His book, *Tunis, Land und Leute*, was released in 1882, both in German and English. Hesse-Wartegg was a writer and traveler by profession. Among his works, one can find travelogues from both "Orient" and North America (Mexico, United States, Canada). The list of his publications reveals his romantic character as well as fascination with adventurous expeditions in poorly populated areas.[11]

Marius Bernard (1847–1914) is the author of a three-part series, describing his journey around the Mediterranean Sea, presented in a 12-volume set. The first series begins with Bernard's description of his trip from Tripoli to Tunis and his travel itinerary includes an area inhabited by Berber ethnic groups in the southwest part of the administrative center of Gabes. Bernard chooses the city of Gabes as the temporary base for his trips around the region – west, towards *Djarra*, south to *Douiret* and the surrounding *ksour*, with a detour to the area surrounding the present-day village of Matmata-ancienne. His travel itinerary provides us with a valuable collection of top-onyms, as many villages no longer exist.[12] The work was published in 1892, a mere 11 years after the French occupation of the "Régence." Yet, in the early 1890s, the governorate of Arad was a consolidated territory of the Protectorate administration. Judging by the complaints made by local residents, which were addressed to the central government in Tunis, "indigenes" managed to acclimatize themselves quickly to the bureaucracy associated with the Protectorate.[13] It should be noted, however, that the Protectorate administration reached only as far as the extent of the network of roads and péages that were being built in order to enhance the infrastructure. During the 1890s, the main issues of communication between the governor of Arad and government headquarters in Tunis were in relation to the construction of new roads and the purchase of land. The absence of a comprehensive road network is also noted in Bernard's accounts, e.g. when he describes the unsuitability of the roads west of Hamma and Gabes.

Records on the author himself are rather limited compared with the records for Lorin and Hesse-Wartegg, yet Bernard could be considered as "child of his times," as a proponent of civilizing mission due to his original interests in colonial world. He graduated in medicine in 1872 with the thesis on Disorders in Nervous System.[14] In next 10 years he published several reports from medical conferences, devoted to the hygiene in and health situation on the colonies.[15] Since 1883 mostly the travelogues and their literary adaptations prevail in his bibliography. He published not only a story of his own journey around the Mediterranean, but one can find also a book on his travel to Indochine.[16]

By the time Bernard appeared in Gabes, the city was a government center of the Arad region, managed by a Consul General.[17] The governor had direct postal links to the north, and as far as Gafsa to the west. Despite the lack of paved roads and highways, the protectorate administration had implemented certain irregular connections with oases and villages in remote *caïdat*s, achieving this through its network of officers and scattered military units. For occasional travelers, a guide setting out the role of an army officer was a necessity. Elsewhere, the pages of logs are full of emotion, sometimes reflecting a state of near despair, especially in relation to the region of Ksars: "At fifteen hundred meters from Ksar rises bordj,[18] erected and occupied by our troops – the only place where Europeans can find refuge."[19]

Lorin's log also contains a description of the character of his guide, originating from the ranks of the army in the person of Commandant Rebillet. In addition to this French officer, the traveling group was supported by a smaller number of *spahi*[20] (former members of beylical units, now under French command). The language skills of travelers, and also of local leaders of the Protectorate, were not adequate to meet the requirements of the indigenous environment in which the journeys took place. Therefore, governors and ministers needed the assistance of interpreters in order to communicate with the local indigenous authorities. We assume that they were mostly recruited from among the local population (the so-called "*Indigenes Armés*"), and incorporated into the colonial army. Lorin provides first hand evidence as part of his report of a visit of Matmata: "The natives . . . started a conversation with our sipahi."[21]

Another issue was the (linguistic) competence of the officers serving in the field, such as Commandant Rebillet or Captain Bichemin. They probably possessed at least partial knowledge of local variations of Arab and Berber because there are several travelogues recording information about their communications with the local population – e.g. Lorin's guide and protector, Lieutenant Rebillet, is responsible for "correcting and – if it is needed – the odd translation" during proceeding a complaint of one caïd from Hadèje, addressed to Ministers of Arad.[22]

In some places travelers mention the languages of particular ethnic groups. From among the travelogues written around the end of the nineteenth century, one brilliant example in the form of an ethnographic-linguistic collection has been preserved – Hans Stumme, in 1899, compiled a set of folklore hymns which originated from the indigenous Berbers of Tamezret village.[23] Although he did not collect data directly in Tamezret, but from Tamezret-born poets living in arabophone Tunis, his accounts provide us with a valuable artifact. Recent research has also revealed that the same folkloric outlines can be found in today's versions of traditional folklore collections in Tamezret.

However, unlike Stumme, most travelers had no formal education in linguistics. This does not invalidate their observations – they might not have been able to produce analytic analyses of the language itself, but they were able to detect the incorrect interpretations of the language, which were characteristic features of the late-romantic period of Berber linguistics. Notes provided by travelers thus remain at the level of statements such as, "Listen to them (the Tuaregs)! They speak Tamaoq, which as a Berber dialect has nothing to do with the language of Arabs and whose origin is hidden in the darkness of the past."[24] The aspect we can rely on is that similar accounts of languages were directly recorded from field observations, thus acting today as a source of largely forgotten endonyms.

"Indigènes" and ethnonymic variations of the late-romantic era

All three books which form the basis of our study devote a substantial portion of the text to the ethnic identity of the population, although it must be noted with regret that more detailed definitions are either missing and different sections of the text are often contradictory. The following passage illustrates an attempt to enumerate at least the most common uses of each etnonym, and to point out its relationship with specific topics, such as customs, dress, and religiosity. In general, based on content analysis, we may determine two main theses: (1) Mentions of ethnicity or race are common features of all investigated sources when speaking about the dichotomy between "Arab" and "non-Arab" phenomena; (2) When speaking about the "Protectorate," or "State," the overall dichotomy is described as the relationship between "indigenes" and "gouvernement," mostly without further specifying ethnicity or a general ethnonym ("berbère," "nègre" etc.).

The environment, which is described in all three investigated sources, was, to a great extent during the time of the French protectorate, culturally and ethnically heterogeneous. Not surprisingly, the authors perceive different "races and tribes" very sympathetically and pay attention to "otherness," sometimes going into incredible detail. Other aspects, such as local religiosity characteristics or Islam, often remain largely ignored.[25] The dichotomy that existed between Arabic and black members of the population is very much a live issue, especially when describing pathways through the village of Mareth (south of Gabes), where Bernard describes the use of the water reservoir. He notes that "blacks" were abusing the water source. In addition, Hesse-Wartegg informs the reader about a variety of miscellaneous disputes and conflicts between the Berbers and the "different Moorish and Arabic races of the Oasis."[26]

As to the issue of Arad, all travelers remain silent in relation to the relative hierarchy of different social groups within society – it can be assumed that the protectorate administration managed to subsume all ethnic segments of the population under the cloak of "civilization" within a relatively short space of time. The division of jurisdiction, as France had introduced in Morocco or Algeria, was largely unknown in this region. An historical analogy may be drawn through reference to the example of Tripoli, where Bernard recorded the existence of the slave trade, even providing accounts of the price of slaves being sold there.[27]

Illustrations of the segregation of black and Arabic people do not appear, with even Wartegg admitting that there was a certain degree of mixing, with the exception of the Chenini Berbers, who, among other things, preserved their language.[28] The mixing of races, the transference of social roles, and the frequently cited degree of mobility, were, in all probability, quite common features. These phenomena do not fit with the stereotypical ideas that travelers often carried with them (and which they usually acquired by reading European "Orientalist" literature). Thus, Bernard is surprised by the example of one Negro ("négrillon"), who claims to be a descendant of the Prophet: "how can a black man be a descendant of Muhammad?"[29]

Although many of the notes in these records may be historically inaccurate, some of them are based on solid foundations, e.g. in relation to the evidence of both the coexistence and conflicts between Arab and Berber ethnic groups in the region. Berbers are still considered as "mountain men" – even in Lorin's and Bernard's writings they often appears only as "Montagnards" – not an uninteresting fact in that many Berbers (mostly Matmati) in the area still refer to themselves as jibaelli (highlanders). When speaking about highlanders, Bernard also mentions the habit of breeding working dogs without precisely specifying the ethnicity of their respective owners. The coexistence of indigenous Berber groups is portrayed in terms of a rural idyll, exemplifying unreserved mutual trust.[30] However, the sword of Damocles still hangs over the tranquil fields of the Berbers as the threat presented by the Arab population is ever present: "Native Berbers against the conquering Arabs."[31] The description of the Berber peasant idyll contrasts with the (often unflattering) image of the laziness and poor working habits of some of the Arabs, who are "tired even before doing anything."[32]

It is worth noting that Protectorate administration itself made considerable effort in classifications of "indigènes." The production was not limited only on internal records, now preserved as archive relicts, but also as printed anthologies, published by authorities. In the search of possible audience one can consider mainly the impact on colonial personnel (both civil and military) in the Protectorate. It is also worth noting that almost one third of French population the Tunisia held a position in protectorate administration; therefore, publications made by authorities such as *"Nomenclature et répartition des Tribus de Tunisie"* (Nomenclature and distribution of Tribes in Tunisia) clearly appeared among a relatively large part of French-speaking colonies.[33]

By the beginning of the twentieth century, the variety of records describing indigenous people of the Protectorate was enriched by scientific approach. Those "colonial" scientists emerged from the need of more detailed knowledge on local populations. One can see the shift from pure "colonial" science into more philological and ethnographical aspect, especially in Algeria. Tunisia was not such a case, but still some efforts were made in descriptions of local language varieties.[34]

Oriental fascination – the "troglodytes"[35] and the *ksar*

The dwellings of Berbers and nomads are a common source of fascination in all travelogues and early ethnographies. Bernard even devotes an entire chapter to *"Gabès et les troglodytes."* When describing Gabès, Hesse-Wartegg admits that it is the most fascinating place in Tunisia. During the visit to Beni-Zelten, Bernard first mentions the "big hole opening up like an empty vessel." On one occasion, Lorin relates that in Matmata he met "natives, emerging from the ground all around us."[36] Underground dwellings, as a source of fascination, become the distinguishing feature of the "Berber" element. The troglodyte dwellings made such an impression on travelers that they were not afraid to compare them to the catacombs! The stark contrast between "us and them," the binary opposition identity, was personified here in the form of two opposing worlds, life on the surface and life below ground. In addition to the colorful descriptions of the "holes," notes were occasionally made in relation to the social dimension of the troglodyte lifestyle.[37]

It is often recorded that when inspecting the troglodyte dwellings, none of the local population were in attendance; therefor the following passage is one of the few that provides us with a record of a visit to a house during the day. One of the most moving parts of Lorin's story is undoubtedly his description of Old Matmata. It is also a quite unique description of daily life in one of the isolated religious schools in Arad.[38] Similarly detailed descriptions are also made by authors writing about Ksar, a fortified refuge. In addition, a number of notes on the social organization of Ksar remain in the texts: granaries were permanently guarded – security guards carried the keys to the common granary constantly with them. In the passage concerning the Ksar area (inhabited by Berber tribes), Bernard almost never mentions the "berbères." He prefers to point out their tribal designation, e.g. "*Matmatî*" (*Ce sont des Matmati, des Troglodytes*), *Dar Kouinet, Hadéje,* and *Toujane*.[39]

The kind of "fascination" seems to be a common and rather necessary aspect of traveler's writing of the time. The perspective reader is always supplied with "fantastic" descriptions from "other world."[40] Fascination of "oriental" element is not limited only on early decades of Protectorate, as even at the very end of colonial empire there are a travel writings providing a full range of "Oriental fascination."[41]

The identity of "nomads"

In making remarks about the "nomads" the French travelers never go into such detail and the reader is provided with little information as to their ethnic identity. Bernard and Lorin very often refer to the nomads in general terms only (i.e. as Arabs or Berbers) or present them only in comparative terms such as settled versus nomadic. The only comprehensive description is found in Hesse-Wartegg's records; however, he further complicates the ethnic distinction by using the ethnonym "Moor." According to his description, we can only assume that he was referring to the settled urban population of Arab-Berber ancestry.

However, the question remains as to the ethnic identity of these "Moors" – especially when considering the fact that Hesse-Wartegg points to their declining numbers in the Gabès region (as well as in other Regency areas) and the fact that they live separately from the Berbers. It should be noted that other examined sources often refer not only to *"indigènes,"* but often also to *"négres"* or *"noirs,"* when speaking about the population living near the city of Gabès. Yet current ethnographic research (carried out by the author since 2012) has revealed additional information: in the Gabès area one can still find enclaves of negroid peoples, living in separate neighborhoods from the Arab population (T'Amdo village).

Folk traditions among Berber groups from the same area have a recurrent motif of the arrival of "Black" or freed slaves "from Libya." Could the "Moors" referred to in a travelogue published in 1882, constitute the residue of indigenous "black" ethnic groups, which previously dominated the coastal area of the later governorate of Arad?

Hesse-Wartegg presents us with another category, which is ignored by other examined French traveler sources – *"Bedouin."* It is difficult to prove that his remarks about the Bedouin tribe, the Urgema, are just one more in a series of mediated references. Wartegg describes the hazards associated with traveling on roads in the coastal areas between Gabès and Sarsis (Zarzis), where there were "no travelers who would not be robbed of everything, including clothing, despite numerous military escorts."[42] The rampaging of "Bedouins" takes place in an area where the local vassal Bey has only limited powers in some districts. Due to the fact that Wartegg's text was written only at the beginning of the period of the formal French protectorate (a dozen or so years before Bernard's and Lorin's travels), it can be assumed that the subsequent consolidation made by protectorate forces was directed only against these Bedouin-nomads, while the rest of the population, composed of Berbers and Arabs and Moors, did not experience any considerable or fundamental socio-economic reversals following the establishment of the Protectorate.

The literary imagination of the French travelers produces a firework display of adjectives by which they describe different ethnic groups, *"Bedouin noir,"*[43] *"villages troglodytes,"*[44] *"Troglodytes de Tatahouine,"*[45] *"les tribus vagabondes,"*[46] *"sahariens indomptables,"*[47] and *"la ville européenne"* vs. *"la ville indigène."*[48] Side notes then reveal the names of the tribes, such as *"Acaras"* or *"Touzzines,"* which were to disappear during the following century as a result of the Bourguibist reforms. The authors of travelogues did not worry about the need to engage in a deeper level of ethnographic research. When they were not able to cite the name of a tribe, they simply referred to them as *"indigènes,"* often referring to them as *"montagnards"* ("highlanders"), and, more often, simply as *"négrillons."* Easy-going tribal designations – such as references to the Imoghas among the Tuareg – contribute to the confusion of identities among individual ethnic groups.

Conclusion

The picture we gain of the indigenous population, based on the investigated sources, reveals a range of similarities, despite the different circumstances of the individuals involved and variations in the overall style of the particular sources. The most striking themes to be considered are the ethnic heterogeneity (evident in the mosaic of relationships between Arabs, Berbers, and Blacks) and a fascination with cultural artifacts. The first area to be mentioned is in relation to the ethnographic aspect (associated with the traveler's amateurish and perhaps unconscious anthropological approach). The second topic relates to the tourist-archaeological aspect. A prerequisite for the identification of themes is the statement that travelers described those topics that were immediately displayed as part of the then-current social reality; travelers tended not to seek out pre-defined topics to guide their writing. This assertion has proved to be valid, due to the absence of many important topics such as local religiosity and ortopraxis. The distinctive picture of the "indigènes," as used in the sources, is either constructed largely on racial grounds (without the specific identification of ethnic identities) or in relation to the place of origin (caused by the absence of data that travelers simply could not obtain).

The "ethnographic" descriptions produced by the travelers reveal a particular image of the ideas associated with the civilizing mission concept. However, the Protectorate has not always been regarded as a civilizing hand, full of glorious objectives. All authors complain about the low levels of morale and the limited ability of the guards who had been recruited from among the locals. This is a reflection of the deeper problem, which was to attract a good deal of attention in the France of the day. The light infantry regiments in Algeria and Tunisia were seen as the horrible outcome of the honorable intentions associated with the "mission civilisatrice," both in a political sense and in ethical terms.

Notes

1 Giovanni Lévi, "On Microhistory," in: *New Perspectives in Historical Writing*, ed. by Peter Burke (State College, PA: Pennsylvania State Press, 1991).
2 George Iggers, *From Macro to Microhistory: The History of Everyday Life* (Hanover: Wesleyan University Press, 1997).
3 Henri Lorin, *Une Promenade en Tunisie* (Paris: Hachette, 1896).
4 Marius Bernard, *De Tripoli à Tunis* (Paris: Librairie Renouard, 1892).
5 Ernst de Hesse-Wartegg, *Tunis – The Land and the People* (New York: Dodd, Mead, and Company, 1882).
6 Henri Lorin, *Une Promenade en Tunisie* (Paris: Hachette, 1896), 529.
7 Bernard Roy spent his life almost exclusively in Tunisia. In the very beginning of his career, he worked as telegraphist in several Tunisian cities and as consular agent in the city of Kef. By the end of the nineteenth century he came into a

high-rank post of secretary-minister. Louis Machuel was outstanding figure of French educational reforms in Tunisia and Morroco.

8 Lorin's writings in the field of "colonial geography" include: *L'Afrique à l'entrée du Vingtième Siècle* (Paris: Augustin Challamel, 1901), *Le Peuplement français de l'Algérie et le Sud-Ouest de la France* (Bordeaux: Imp. J. Durand, 1903), or *La France puissance coloniale: Étude d'histoire et de géographie politiques* (Paris: Augustin Challamel, 1906).

9 La quinzaine colonial, 25/3/1902.

10 Henri Lorin, "En Tunisie: Le port de Sfax," *Questions politiques et coloniales*, 1 (1896), 356.

11 His publishing activity seems to be enormous. Between 1874 and 1902, he had been publishing new book every one or two years.

12 With care, descriptions of places such as *Chenini, Menzel, Temoulbou, Marap, El-Hamdi, SidiBou'l Baba, Bordj-el-Hamma, Debaheha* are recorded. In addition, records are made of the road between Gabes and Mareth: Teboulba, 'Oued-Merzig, Del-Hamdi' and Oued-Zerkine; the road to Medenine: the area around Djebel-N'fouça (Jebel Nafusa); the peaks of the massif Tadjera; and the village of M'tameur. dTaT, 70.

13 Les archives nationales de Tunisie, serie G-H.

14 Marius Bernard, *Quelques considérations sur les rétentions d'urine dans les lésions et les affections du système nerveux* (Paris: L. Cristin, 1872).

15 Marius Bernard, *Constitution médicale de Cannes pendant l'année 1881–1882. note sur la fièvre typhoïde* (Paris: Impr. De L. Vincent, 1882).

16 Marius Bernard, *De Toulon au Tonkin* (Paris: Laplace, Sanchez, 1885).

17 Allegro was installed by the commander of the French intervention in 1881, General Logerot (Conststant-Balluet, 1891), 256.

18 Bordj (ar.) – (lit.) tower; small stronghold.

19 Marius Bernard, *De Tripoli à Tunis* (Paris: Librairie Renouard, 1892), 89.

20 The name comes from the Ottoman "Sipahi," i.e. Rider.

21 Henri Lorin, "En Tunisie: Le port de Sfax," *Questions politiques et coloniales*, 1 (1896), 561.

22 Ibid.

23 Hans Stumme, *Märchen der Berbern von Tamazratt* (Leipzig: J. R. Hinrichs, 1990).

24 Marius Bernard, *De Tripoli à Tunis* (Paris: Librairie Renouard, 1892), 26.

25 The cited text is enriched by Chapon's drawing of a "Black beggar" ("*un mendiantnègre*"). dTaT, p. 21.

26 Ernst de Hesse-Wartegg, *Tunis – The Land and the People* (New York: Dodd, Mead, and Company, 1882), 275.

27 Marius Bernard, *De Tripoli à Tunis* (Paris: Librairie Renouard, 1892), 23.

28 Ernst de Hesse-Wartegg, *Tunis – The Land and the People* (New York: Dodd, Mead, and Company, 1882), 275.

29 Marius Bernard, *De Tripoli à Tunis* (Paris: Librairie Renouard, 1892), 80.

30 Henri Lorin, "En Tunisie: Le port de Sfax," *Questions politiques et coloniales*, 1 (1896), 564.

31 Ibid., 556.

32 Marius Bernard, *De Tripoli à Tunis* (Paris: Librairie Renouard, 1892), 63.

33 Sécretariat general du gouvernement tunisien, *Nomenclature et répartition des Tribus de Tunisie* (Chalon-sur-Saone: Impr. française et orientale, 1900).

34 One the very first is Shammkh, Ibrahm Motylinski and Adoplhe G. Calassanti, *Le Djebel Nefousa. Transcripstion, traduction française et notes avec une étude grammatical* (Paris: Ernest Leroux, 1898).

35 In the examined sources, the word "Troglodyte" is used freely both for people and the cave dwellings itself. French authors from the late nineteenth century often confuse the two meanings, while local vernacular has a strict terms for both dwellings and their inhabitants.

36 Henri Lorin, "En Tunisie: Le port de Sfax," *Questions politiques et coloniales*, 1 (1896), 561.

37 Marius Bernard, *De Tripoli à Tunis* (Paris: Librairie Renouard, 1892), 85.

38 Henri Lorin, "En Tunisie: Le port de Sfax," *Questions politiques et coloniales*, 1 (1896), 569.

39 Marius Bernard, *De Tripoli à Tunis* (Paris: Librairie Renouard, 1892), 84.

40 For more detailed explication see Mohammad Gharipour and Nilay Özlü, *The City in the Muslim World: Depictions by Western Travel Writers* (London: Routledge, 2015).

41 Ali Behadad, *Belated Travelers: Orientalism in the Age of Colonial Dissolution* (Durham and London: Duke University Press, 1994).

42 Ernst de Hesse-Wartegg, *Tunis – The Land and the People* (New York: Dodd, Mead, and Company, 1882), 276.

43 Marius Bernard, *De Tripoli à Tunis* (Paris: Librairie Renouard, 1892), 67.

44 Henri Lorin, "En Tunisie: Le port de Sfax," *Questions politiques et coloniales*, 1 (1896), 561.

45 Marius Bernard, *De Tripoli à Tunis* (Paris: Librairie Renouard, 1892), 91.

46 Ibid., 27.

47 Ibid.

48 Ibid., 68.

6 Ruanda-Urundi under Belgian control

Demography, labor force, and migration

Jan Záhořík

Introduction

Rwanda and Burundi (colonial Ruanda-Urundi) became German colonies in 1885 during the Scramble for Africa but only a limited attention had been paid to the development of these remote areas as German East Africa (later Tanganyika) or Cameroon were valued more for their access to the sea and further economic potential. Such lack of German interest in landlocked countries in Equatorial Africa can be well documented on the example of Heinrich Schnee's (former German Governor) influential book published in 1926, where almost no space is given to Ruanda-Urundi.[1] During World War I, Germany lost its colonies which were then divided among the Allied Powers on the basis of the Treaty of Versailles in 1919. Since the very first battles in East Africa, a question of partitioning and administering the German colonies became acute. From the very beginning, Great Britain and Belgium were the only countries to take control of German East African territories. Since 1916 until 1919, Great Britain still tried to find a way to overtake both Tanganyika and Ruanda-Urundi, as the British proposed a creation of a unified administrative system in former German East African colonies which would directly lead to the British colonial rule.[2]

Finally, the Belgian mandate over territories of Rwanda and Burundi came out of Article 119 of the Treaty of Versailles, signed on 28 June 1919, on whose basis Germany gave up any claims and demands on former colonies for the benefit of the Allied Powers. On 18 April 1923, Belgium signed the Charter of the League of Nations by which Brussels confirmed the mandate and responsibility over the territory. On 20 October 1924, Ruanda-Urundi was proclaimed a mandate of Class C, which meant the country would have no opportunity for gaining any king of autonomy. The Mandates underwent occasional inspection by the League officials to ensure that the territory was governed with a humanitarian approach. The administration of Ruanda-Urundi was thus completely in the hands of Belgium which had to rule the country in concordance with interests of other members of the League of Nations, and with respect and on behalf of the local populations.[3] In 1925 Ruanda-Urundi was administratively attached to the Belgian Congo, and the Royal decree from 11 January 1926 clarified the special regime of rule over Ruanda-Urundi. In this chapter, I will focus particularly on specific issues of demography, migration, and labor force which the Belgians had to solve since the early 1920s until 1950s. For these purposes I use statistical data found in Belgian Archives or literature to explore the studied issue.

Demography and labor force in Ruanda-Urundi

Colony of Ruanda-Urundi was inhabited mainly by agriculturalists Bahutu, pastoralists Batutsi, and hunters-gatherers Batwa. Bahutu formed a vast majority of people (85%), while Batutsi (14%) and Batwa (1%) were minorities.[4] These groups had to be governed by indirect rule, as proclaimed and defended by Pierre Ryckmans, Urundi's resident and later Congo governor at the early 1920s.[5] Since the 1920s, Belgians in Ruanda-Urundi were confronted with significant troubles and problems including famine caused by the war. Official Belgian reports from 1928 and 1929 spoke about potential food crises in several localities, namely Kasenda and Musenyi, as well as Kasongwe. This was nothing new as early reports on Rwanda included mentions concerning potential famine caused by long-lasting drought which periodically broke out in the following decades, as witnessed by Belgian officials in 1921–1922 and 1926. With the development of Belgian administration, diversification of cash crops evolved which had certain impact also on food security of Ruanda-Urundi. Among significant crops we may include potatoes, which soon became the main competitor to the then dominant sorghum. Similarly, there was a remarkable development of production of rice, soya, and many other kinds of crops.[6]

In both Rwanda and Burundi, Belgians had to gain sympathies and collaboration of local elites in order to develop the system of forced labor by which the colonies differed from the Belgian Congo or neighboring British Territories in East Africa. Political and administrative reforms were thus concerted actions with the Catholic Church playing an important role of a "civilizing mission." Many local chiefs were sympathetic and loyal to Belgians while in some parts of the colony, occasional revolts occurred.[7] Development of Belgian administration and the indirect rule, on the other hand, caused continual marginalization of the power of *mwami* (king) and local chiefs, and provoked ethnic categorization and fixation of ethnic identities (Hutu, Tutsi, Twa).[8] Though *mwami* was traditionally perceived as a person responsible for the well-being of the state and its people and for redistribution of wealth, the mwami's position did not allow him to enrich himself. It was in 1903 when the beginning of destabilization of traditional political (as well as economic) structure took place. A Treaty of Kiganda, signed on 6 June 1903 between mwami Mwezi Gisabo and German representatives, put previously unseen limitations to the power of the king in Burundi (similar treaties were signed also in Rwanda). Spread of the influence of White Fathers and elimination of royal symbols' importance prevailed until the Belgian mandated rule.[9] Missions played a remarkable role not only in evangelization of the colonies but they had a significant economic impact, especially in the Congo.[10]

One of the crucial aspects of economy that already the Germans had to face was the lack of infrastructure connecting Rwanda and Burundi with important trade centers on the East African coast. Though we have certain knowledge about economic as well as political ties between Rwanda and Burundi and the Eastern parts of the Congo already in pre-colonial times,[11] trade routes between the two landlocked countries and the coastal areas especially in Tanzania existed with more or less dubious security. At the beginning of the twentieth century, still under German rule, several routes flourished while other suffered from changes in export of commodities. Bukoba, one of the main ports on the East African coast of that time, received huge quantities of goods, mainly skins, from both Rwanda and Burundi.[12] The Belgian rule, as we will see later, with the system of forced labor, introduced some new elements in commercial relations between Ruanda-Urundi and Tanganyika (former German East Africa), as besides agricultural products, thousands of Burundians and Rwandans left their homelands in order to search for and obtain better opportunities for their livelihood.

Belgians, in order to fully develop their system of production of cash crops, needed to have a detailed idea about the number of local population and especially the so-called HAV – *Hommes Adultes Valides,* or able-bodied man. Until 1924 it was almost impossible to conduct a census due to the lack of skilled personnel and existence of other acute priorities. After the beginning of 1925, the Belgian administration was able to propose more and more precise estimates as the most valid collected data came from the Christian communities where numbers of baptisms, deaths, and marriages formed the core of the register. Christianization of natives was one of the major components and central issues of Belgian colonialism and the role of Catholic Church increased in the following decades.[13] Despite such an improvement it was still not possible to make results applicable on the whole population of Ruanda-Urundi. For instance, a report from 1926 stated that in the mountains, number of births was very high; population census in Rugori (Ngozi) showed 288 living children in the age from three years per 202 women. Birthrate was 47 children per 100 women. Death rate was low and could be compared to the European average. The Vicar Apostolic of Urundi mentioned a death rate he had witnessed at around 8 percent in the first year of life. Death rate at later age was significantly higher than in Europe.

In 1927, population census was conducted on eight selected hills, and to the number of 480 000 inhabitants, a factor 4 435 was attached. Overall population estimate resulted in the number of 2 128 000 inhabitants.[14] Population estimates in the 1920s were decreasing from year to year. While in 1924, Belgians estimated some three million of indigenous inhabitants, in 1927 and 1928 it was 2 128 000 and in 1930 only 1 732 355.[15]

Population censuses became more precise in the following decades, and from 1940s and 1950s we have sufficient data concerning the indigenous populations. Table 6.1 shows structure of population in chefferies and outside chefferies.[16]

As noted in Table 6.2, among Belgian subjects in Equatorial Africa, Batutsi enjoyed the highest status as these "Nilotic" people were regarded "intelligent" and thus closer to "civilization" than the Bantu including Bahutu and all the Congolese people.[17] Despite these "racial" prejudices, and despite the process of ethnic categorization which had begun at the early phase of European colonization of Ruanda-Urundi, some Belgians admitted that both Bahutu and Batutsi enjoyed the same values including language, cultural traits, and habits, as written by former Governor of Ruanda-Urundi Jean-Paul Harroy.[18] Although Rwanda and Burundi are landlocked countries and during colonial times they played only a minor role in Belgian colonialism, it attracted many foreigners not only from Asia (Table 6.3) but also a significant number from Europe (Tables 6.4, 6.5, and 6.6), who worked there as state administrators, advisors, teachers, missionaries, instructors, or civil servants.

Table 6.1 Indigenous populations in Ruanda-Urundi

Ruanda: Population des chefferies (statistiques des Administrateurs de Territoire)
Population of chiefdoms (statistics of Territorial Administrators)

Men	Women	Boys	Girls	Total
501 070	584 229	637 977	636 957	2 360 233

Urundi: Population des chefferies (Population of chiefdoms)

Men	Women	Boys	Girls	Total
455 301	511 126	484 214	517 121	1 967 762

Ruanda: Population non soumise au régime des chefferies (Population non-subject to the regime of chiefdoms)

Men	Women	Boys	Girls	Total
5 419	3 733	3 815	3 558	16 525

Urundi: Population non soumise au régime des chefferies (Population non-subject to the regime of chiefdoms)

Men	Women	Boys	Girls	Total
16 900	14 137	10 792	10 642	52 471

Total population of Ruanda-Urundi in 1955 was 4 396 991 (Ruanda: 2 376 758; Urundi: 2 020 233); in 1952, it was 4 035 123.

Table 6.2 Estimate of percent representation of "races" in the colony, 1952[19]

	Ruanda	Urundi	Ruanda-Urundi
Batutsi	17,5%	12,14%	14,95%
Bahutu	81,52%	86,16%	83,73%
Batwa	0,98%	1,70%	1,32%

Table 6.3 Foreigners in Ruanda-Urundi in 1956: Asians by sex

Nationality	Men	Women	Total
Arabs	591	544	1135
British (East Africa and Zanzibar)	258	257	515
Pakistanis	249	191	440
Indians	179	136	315
Others	33	33	66
Total	1 310	1 161	2 471

Table 6.4 Foreigners in Ruanda-Urundi in 1956: Europeans

Nationality	1952	1953	1954
Belgian	3 738	3 991	4 110
Greek	374	404	394
Italian	156	158	178
French	156	138	170
British	123	118	122
Dutch	102	94	110
American	108	133	100
Other	364	370	375
Total	5 121	5 406	5 559

Table 6.5 Total population of foreigners

Category	1952	1953	1954
Black population	4 101 841	4 144 000	4 260 933
European population	5 121	5 406	5 559
Asian population	1 997	2 145	2 471
Mulattos and mestizos	1 328	946	942
Total	4 110 287	4 152 497	4 269 905

Source: Bulletin de la Banque Centrale du Congo Belge et du Ruanda-Urundi 5 (1), January 1956.

Table 6.6 Foreigners in Ruanda-Urundi by number, 25 April 1946

Germans	26	Russians	14
Americans	42	Swedes	23
British	78	Swiss	19
Belgians	1 254	South Africans	11
Austrians	2	Turks	9
Canadians	1	Palestinians	2
Danish	12	Other Europeans	20
Frenchmen	65	Mulattos	202
Greek	127	Ethiopians	1
Dutch	47	Arabs	524
Hungarians	3	Afghans	17
Italians	57	Baluchis	36
Luxemburg	22	Hindus	759
Portuguese	39	Senegalese	61
Polish	8	Other	465

Source: La Population du Ruanda-Urundi, No 636/XXVI-3, 25 April 1946, AA/AI (4378), no 82.

As noted in Table 6.4 and Table 6.6, Asiatic population in Ruanda-Urundi tended to grow from year to year. In 1945, 718 Hindus, 528 Arabs, 37 Baluchis, and 20 Afghanis have lived there while only 49 Senegalese and 1 Habesha formed the tiny African non-indigenous minority. Asians had been traditionally present since the early twentieth century in East and South Africa as merchants and entrepreneurs and Ruanda-Urundi was no different. Some 266 merchants and 79 commercial agents lived there in 1945. Among almost 2 000 Asians, 60 worked in Usumbura and Kigali as clerks and 29 as chauffeurs. As in coastal areas of Kenya or South Africa, many Indians owned their private business companies and generally their role in colonial economy was important.[20] Because of their importance, their number grew continually through the 1950s. Because we know that significant number of Asian citizens were women, we can conclude that whole families moved from the Indian subcontinent to Equatorial Africa and thus it was a coherent movement, not a spontaneous one.

The role of Asians was not limited only to commerce since, according to Belgian official documents, Asians were recommended for their loyalty and intelligence as well as "civilization." At the end of the World War II, almost 5 000 Muslims lived in Ruanda while more than 10 000 in Urundi. Due to permanent settlement of Muslim communities, 24 Islamic schools with almost 1 000 pupils existed in 1940s in major towns of the colony. Their organization was a matter of many disputes and critiques, but their existence was entirely a subject of local religious communities and received no aid or assistance from the government.

Migration to and from Ruanda-Urundi

People from Ruanda-Urundi, especially from Urundi, tended to leave the country to search for better paid job opportunities in neighboring Tanganyika, or the Belgian Congo.[21] Although officially Ruanda-Urundi was a mandated territory and not a "colony," Belgians sought to use the country as the source of income and agricultural production. In this sense, nothing changed until 1959 when Ruanda-Urundi and Belgian Congo became controlled by a Minister of Belgian Congo and Ruanda-Urundi, and both colonies were given certain liberation programs. Until the end of the 1950s, labor force was strictly controlled by Belgians.[22]

A remarkable number of Asian workers settled not only in Ruanda-Urundi but especially in British colonies in East Africa. Though it was South Africa which hosted the majority of Indian and Indonesian population from the end of the nineteenth century due to both Dutch and British economic engagement,[23] it was East Africa which had had the longest relations with the world of Islam and the longest experience with foreign Muslim populations. Historical contacts with Arab and Persian traders and recent early twentieth-century labor migration from South-East Africa were the main ways of spreading Islam not only in Tanzania, but in the Great Lakes region as well.[24]

The flow of immigrants from Asia remained constant for decades and in official Belgian reports they were valued for their peacefulness and trading skills. As the number of Muslims among these immigrants grew, the first Muslim mosque was built in Usumbura in 1930s. Although the majority of Asians professed Islam, a number of Hinduists could be found in Usumbura as well. Importance of immigrants only increased during the World War II.[25]

Interestingly, the population of both Europeans and Asians increased remarkably during the World War II, with the number of Europeans almost doubling from 1940 to 1944 and so did the number of Asians, including more than 700 Indians and more than 500 Arabs. Belgian statistical data also includes numbers of the so-called colored and mulatos.[26]

As already mentioned, a significant number of migrants from Ruanda-Urundi sought work in British territories or Belgian Congo and due to better work conditions, a larger portion of Rwandese and Burundese migrants chose Tanganyika or Uganda as their final destinations. Migration to neighboring countries had to be seen in two ways, as a spontaneous migration and as directed migration.

Remarkable development of plantations in Tanganyika or Eastern Congo inspired thousands of inhabitants of Ruanda-Urundi to undergo a spontaneous migration in hope to find better paid jobs than in their countries of origin. Such a migration only increased with the beginning of the World War II and there were several waves of immigrants, with the first heading to North Kivu and to a lesser extent to Katanga where the mining industry flourished from 1920s to 1940s and attracted attention of many foreigners.[27] Another group of migrants came directly to the border town of Bukavu which became known for its "cosmopolitan" and ethnically diverse atmosphere. During the World War II years, some 12 000 people from Ruanda-Urundi entered the town of Bukavu.

The flow of migrants to British East Africa was even more dependent on spontaneity as dozens of thousands of Rwandese and Burundians, as shown in Table 6.7, took the opportunity to find a sufficient seasonal work. Besides Belgian Congo and Tanganyika, there was a far less public but comparably important relationship between Ruanda-Urundi and Uganda, another British colony. It was especially the World War II which highlighted "some discomforting characteristics of Uganda's economic life."[28] Uganda's economy became heavily dependent on labor force from outside, especially from Ruanda-Urundi, and unlike Belgians in their territories, the British proved to be unable to control the mass movement of migrants. Such movements resulted in British refusal to guarantee public order in places of mass presence of foreign migrants. According to some contemporaries, annually approximately 100 000 migrants came to Uganda, most of whom had their origin in Ruanda. These migrants sought to meet Belgian tax obligations as Uganda offered more work opportunities than Ruanda-Urundi.[29] Rwandan seasonal migrants worked under Indian or European employers, mainly in cotton and sugar industry. Similar labor exchange took place between Belgian Congo and Tanganyika in both directions.[30]

In the prewar period, a spontaneous migration to British East Africa was a dominant feature of migrant labor movements in Belgian colonies. Despite Belgian tendencies to document and control any labor force movements within Ruanda-Urundi, labor conditions and larger number of well-paid job opportunities forced seasonal workers to cross the borders to Tanganyika

Table 6.7 Migration from Burundi to the Belgian Congo and the British Territories

Year	To Belgian Congo	To the British Territories
1949	3 379	16 543
1950	4 601	11 470
1951	4 470	10 182
1952	4 831	9 275
1953	610	13 298
1954	1 600	16 405
1955	1 086	28 113
1956	619	25 901

Source: Bulletin de la Banque Centrale du Congo Belge et du Ruanda-Urundi 5 (1), January 1956.

and other regions. The reason of increased economic migration could be seen also in the development and economic stabilization of agricultural and industrial sectors of British colonies in the prewar period, and in the enormous growth of mining industry not only in Eastern Congo.[31]

Directed, or controlled, migration from Ruanda-Urundi was encouraged by concrete institutions, and permission to work outside one's homeland region was given individually to each person for temporary period, although a small number of migrants could gain long-term permission as well. Temporary migration was directed primarily to Belgian Congo and in lesser extent to British East Africa as the Belgians needed to support their mining industry by cheap labor force on non-Congolese. Lack of labor force in Kivu and Katanga in prewar period still coincided with brutal genocidal rule of Leopold II, under whose reign the number of Congolese population decreased from 20 million in 1878 to 6 million in 1908 and the loss of population seriously affected primarily these central and eastern regions of the Congo.[32]

In the Belgian Congo, the labor recruitment was effectively operated by Union Minière du Haut-Katanga on the basis of serious studies concerning not only the needs of their mining fields but also the acclimatization and psychology of indigenous populations of Ruanda-Urundi.[33] Another destination of workers within controlled migration was the region of Kivu in Eastern Congo where several Belgian companies sought to employ workers from Ruanda-Urundi in order to fill their staffs. Migration towards Tanganyika and other territories in British East Africa was, as suggested, more a matter of spontaneous migration although small numbers of workers were sent there to build roads and infrastructure.[34] It can be said that the most prevalent trend especially in prewar period was the spontaneous migration from Ruanda-Urundi to British East Africa, as shown in Table 6.8. Directed migration was largely used to promote the mining industry in Belgian Congo, while spontaneous migration was used more by seasonal agricultural workers and less by employees in industry.

Already since 1927, the Belgian authorities studied any possibilities of the best utilization of labor force and its economic effects on both sides of

Table 6.8 Migration from Ruanda-Urundi in the 1950s

Country of migration	1953			1954		
	Ruanda	Urundi	Total	Ruanda	Urundi	Total
Belgian Congo	3 851	610	4 461	3 020	1 600	4 620
British East Africa	16 181	13 298	29 479	17 548	16 405	33 953
Total	20 032	13 908	33 940	20 568	18 005	38 573

Congo/Ruanda-Urundi border. Creation of common administrative shelter for both colonies was principally a step toward easier migration of labor force from one country to another. In May 1927, the governmental commission studied possibilities of migration of the Rwandese to Lake Mokoto in Nord Kivu and Burundians to Itombwe in South Kivu. In 1929, Ruanda-Urundi encouraged migrants by launching a program which guaranteed medical preparation to voluntary workers.

In 1939, the government of Kivu tried to implement another project concerning the support of migrants from Ruanda-Urundi, which had to be placed at Fizi at the Lake Tanganyika but this program was not successful. To the contrary, in 1936, it is documented that 600 families from Rwanda settled at Gishari in North-Kivu, which was followed by Rwandese *mwami* who, accompanied by local chiefs, sought for better conditions for these labor migrants. Finally, at the end of 1938, almost 500 men, 267 women, and 560 children found permanent homes at Gishari where they cultivated free land. At the end of 1954, there lived 15 424 families, including more than 60 thousand individuals from Rwanda in Belgian Congo where the majority of these new settlers cultivated and tilled the land and formed the basis for further migration of both Hutu and Tutsi.[35]

Despite a strong regulations and control over labor force, inhabitants of Ruanda-Urundi, facing the fact of forced labor and high taxes in their homelands, used many opportunities to find sufficient employments in neighboring countries. For colonial administration, labor migration was on one hand a necessity (especially in the case of Asian traders coming from India and labor workers coming from Ruanda-Urundi to mining fields in Kivu and Katanga), on the other hand, Belgians sought to create limits for these workers in order to prevent mass and uncontrolled migration which could threaten their own colonial economy.

Notes

1 Heinrich Schnee, *German Colonization: Past and Future – The Truth About the German Colonies* (New York: Alfred A. Knopf, 1926).
2 Cecile Boonet, *Le Ruanda-Urundi: Naissance et Organisation d'un Territoire à Mandat*. Dissertation (Groupe: Histoire, Faculté de Philosophie et Lettres, Université Libre de Bruxelles, 1977), 106.
3 Patrick Manning, *Francophone Sub-Saharan Africa 1880–1995* (Cambridge: Cambridge University Press, 1995), 66.
4 José Clément, "Le Ruanda-Urundi et la Tutelle belge," in: *La colonisation belge. Une grande aventure*, ed. by Gérard Jacques et al. (Bruxelles: Blanchart, 2006), 335.
5 Jean-Pierre Chrétien, *The Great Lakes of Africa: Two Thousand Years of History* (Cambridge, MA: The MIT Press, 2003), 267.
6 Firmin Kinigi, *Realisations économiques de la Belgique au Rwanda et au Burundi pendant les vingt premiéres anées de son administraton (1920–1940)* (Louvain: Université Catholique de Louvain, 1971), 76–88.

7 Augustin Nsanze, *Un Domaine Royal au Burundi. Mbuye (env. 1850–1945)* (Bujumbura: Société Française d'Histoire des Outre-Mers, 1980), 61–66.

8 Augustin Nsanze, *Le Burundi Ancien. L'économie du Pouvoir de 1875 à 1920* (Paris: L'Harmattan, 2001), 296–299.

9 Augustin Nsanze, *Le Burundi Contemporain. L'État-nation en question (1956–2002)* (Paris: L'Harmattan, 2003), 10–20.

10 Jean Stengers, *Congo mythes et réalités. 100 and d'histoire* (Paris: Duculot, 1989), 191–193.

11 David Newbury, *Kings and Clans: Ijwi Island and the Lake Kivu Rift, 1780–1840* (Madison: University of Wisconsin Press, 1991).

12 Jean-Pierre Chrétien, *The Great Lakes of Africa: Two Thousand Years of History* (Cambridge, MA: The MIT Press, 2003), 257.

13 Fortunatus Rudakemwa, *L'évangelisation du Rwanda* (Paris: L'Harmattan, 2005).

14 Daniel Nyambariza, "A Demographic Approach to Colonial Burundi, From Administrative Documents, 1896–1960," in: *Demography from Scanty Evidence: Central Africa in the Colonial Era*, ed. by Bruce Fetter (Boulder and London: Lynne Rienner Publishers, 1990), 101–103.

15 Ibid., 106.

16 Archives Africaines/Affaires Indigenes (AA/AI), Archive of the Ministry of Foreign Affairs, Brussels. (4378), no 82, Structure de la Population par Territoire, Populace Ruanda-Urundi 1955.

17 Isidore Ndaywel É Nziem, *Congo. De l'héritage ancien à la République Démocratique* (Paris: Duculot, 1998), 471.

18 Jean-Paul Harroy, *Rwanda. De la Féodalité á la Démocratie 1955–1962* (Bruxelles: Hayez, 1984), 31.

19 AA/AI (4378), no 82, Note Relative au Document ST/SOA/SerA/15 Intitule "La population du Ruanda-Urundi."

20 AA/AI (4378), no 82. Service d'Information: Asiatiques et Musulmanes au Ruanda-Urundi, B/M No 416, 3 May, 1945.

21 Daniel Nyambariza, "A Demographic Approach to Colonial Burundi, From Administrative Documents, 1896–1960," in: *Demography From Scanty Evidence: Central Africa in the Colonial Era*, ed. by Bruce Fetter (Boulder and London: Lynne Rienner Publishers, 1990), 111.

22 Ch. Didier Gondola, *The History of Congo* (Westport: Greenwood Publishing Group, 2002), 109.

23 Robert C. H. Shell, "Islam in Southern Africa, 1652–1998," in: *The History of Islam in Africa*, ed. by Nehemia Levtzion and Randall L. Pouwels (Oxford: James Currey, 2000), 327–348.

24 See e.g. Lawrence E. Y. Mbogoni, *The Cross vs. The Crescent: Religion and Politics in Tanzania. From the 1890s to the 1990s* (Dar es Salaam: Mkuki na Nyota Publishers, 1998).

25 La Population non-indigene du Ruanda-Urundi pendant la guerre B/M No 626/XXVI, 23 January 1946.

26 Bulletin de la Banque Centrale du Congo Belge et du Ruanda-Urundi 5 (1), January 1956.

27 Jacques Depelchin, *From the Congo Free State to Zaire (1885–1974): Towards a Demystification of Economic and Political History* (London: Codesria, 1992), 34–64.

28 Gardner Thompson, *Governing Uganda: British Colonial Rule and Its Legacy* (Kampala: Fountain Publisher, 2003), 182.

29 Ibid., 183.

30 Gérard Jacques, *Lualaba. Histoires de l'Afrique profonde* (Bruxelles: Racine, 1995), 138–139.

31 Bulletin de la Banque Centrale du Congo Belge et du Ruanda-Urundi 5 (1), January 1956, 4–7.

32 For more information on Leopold's Congo, see Adam Hochschild, *King Leopold's Ghost: A Story of Greed, Terror, and Heroism in Colonial Africa* (Boston: Houghton Mifflin, 1999) and/or Georges Nzongola-Ntalaja, *The Congo from Leopold to Kabila: A People's History* (London and New York: Zed Books, 2003).

33 Bulletin de la Banque Centrale du Congo Belge et du Ruanda-Urundi 5 (1), January 1956.

34 Ibid.

35 Ibid., 4–7.

7 British colonial policy toward Bechuanaland, Basutoland, and Swaziland

Real periphery of peripheries or the Suez of the South?

Linda Piknerová

Introduction

The south of Africa has traditionally represented one of the crucial geographical locations in the world since the times of the beginning of European colonial expeditions or more precisely since the times of the arrival of Dutch colonists. After Dutch settled down in the area surrounding Cape Town during the sixteenth and seventeenth century, the Cape of Good Hope has become the support point for spreading European dominance within southern Africa. Another milestone in the history of "the South" occurred with the Napoleonic Wars at the beginning of nineteenth century, when the "old continent" was wrestling with anarchy and the absence of balance of power. In that times, the Cape of Good Hope belonged to the main "choke points" governed (in fact) by British Empire, which used local navy route for the expansion if its colonial legacy in Asia and Africa. The expansion achieved by Dutch caught the attention of Britain, which joined the second wave of colonialism together with France. Through the cooperation with Dutch settlers, Great Britain expanded to Asia where the "pearl" of the British Empire (British India) was situated. After the outbreak of Napoleonic Wars, Great Britain suffered from the fear of the loss of its hegemony in the southern Atlantic Ocean and suspected France of its hunger for British colonial positions in the Eastern hemisphere. The fearful reaction of the British, alarmed that European Napoleonic Wars could affect non-European areas too, was quite quick and understandable. As the menace of French expansion was felt by British politics, Great Britain occupied the Cape of Good Hope and the former Dutch colony Cape became the key building block of British African policy. Evidently, British interest in the Cape of Good Hope was driven by two aspects: the first one was related to the British ambitions in Asia; the second one was concerned in British African activities pulled by the travellers, adventurers, and policymakers.

While the colonization in the beginning of the nineteenth century was in the name of the conquest of Cape Town, forthcoming decades shown that not only coastal areas could be interesting and the activities of "Whites" looked towards the inland African spaces. As the nineteenth century showed, southern African inland offered enormous riches for everyone who had courage to explore it. In the view of the fact that Great Britain supported a form of colonialism drawn by individuals, southern Africa represented the best place where everyone could have found the best. While the British activities towards the Republic of South Africa are widely known, this chapter aims to show three African inland regions which could be labeled as marginal. Although Bechuanaland, Basutoland, and Swaziland belonged to the British Empire from the end of the nineteenth century to the 1960s, their position in the empire was extremely specific and influenced by the ability of local political elites to cooperate with the British government.[1] Contrary to other British African territories, Bechuanaland, Basutoland, and Swaziland gained the status of protectorate and enjoyed a good reputation in the British Empire´s architecture.[2] With regard to this fact, it seems to us highly relevant to think about British motives underlining this exception. The British approach to Bechuanaland, Basutoland, and Swaziland was deeply influenced by local political conditions as well as wider British colonial ambitions.

British presence in Africa

Needless to say, British colonial policy represents one of the most powerful phenomena in modern age which has been explored by many prominent historians. With caution, Britain entered the era of colonial expansion during the seventeenth century when Navigation Acts were adopted by England. Based on such laws, English shipping companies started to spread around the non-European World. Esprit of freedom, support to liberalism, and faith in freedom of market presented the crucial building blocks of the boom of British colonial expansion having its peak at the turn of nineteenth and twentieth century. Former Colonial Secretary of the British government Joseph Chamberlain wanted all countries in the British Empire to work together and was proud of the fact that he governed the biggest and most populated empire in the world. British present in Africa contributed to the grandness of the empire in many ways.[3]

As already noted, British presence in the South of Africa was motivated by the effort to protect key choke point – Cape Town. Having a look on the map of southern Africa, we realize that there is no similar place like the Cape of Good Hope with such a specific location sheltered by cliffs and a huge bay with a lighthouse at the top of the hill. Famous are memories of sailors remembering how the way from Europe to "the East" was stressful and how happy they were as soon as they saw the Table Mountain with a close harbor standing like an oasis in the middle of nothing. British presence in the African south must be understood in the wider context of European colonialism. During the first wave of colonialism, Portugal explored coastal lines of modern-day Mozambique and Angola, which became an integral part of Portuguese empire after loss of territory in South America. Thinking about the importance of Cape Town, we realize that its annexation was not anything new in British colonial approach and the capture of choke points belonged to the pillars of British strategic thinking. Analogous to Cape Town, Britain aimed to gain control of Suez Canal, in order to gain control of a couple islands in Mediterranean area (e.g. Malta, Cyprus).[4]

In contrast to France, the Netherlands or Portugal, Britain distinguished among different kinds of approach towards occupied areas resulting in the creation of variety of patterns of dependency. This situation had a strong connection with two major facts: (1) different *time of colonization* of particular areas; (2) different *importance of particular areas*. Firstly the fact that the colonization was taking place in various times had its roots in the nature of British Empire, which changed its size since the sixteenth century. As empire extended across the world, new places were incorporated and step by step they found the empire.[5] Secondly, Britain recognized different kinds of dependencies according to their importance for the Empire. The British Empire was comprised of: (1) dominions that had the highest level of autonomy and based on the 1926 Imperial Conference they were granted a special status within the Empire. Following this status, they were treated as autonomous communities in no respect surrogate or inferior to Great Britain. A total amount of six dominions (Canada, Australia, New Zealand, Newfoundland, The Irish Free State, and the South-African Union) acquired the right to create their own laws. (2) colonies including some African, American, and Asian parts they de facto stood for an abbreviation of "Colony not possessing a responsible Government." A specific category unto itself were Crown Colonies, i.e. particular regions in which the Crown maintained control over the legislative. (3) protectorates (including, besides Bechuanaland, Basutoland, and Swaziland, some parts in the Arab World and South East Asia) (4) mandates created after the World War I thanks to a decision of League of Nations; and (5) territories (e.g. including islands in the Caribbean sea).[6] Except the above-mentioned kinds of subordinated areas, India enjoyed an exclusive role confirmed in 1876 when it gained the status of empire. Sudan and New Hebrides gained the status of condominium, which refers to the sharing administration of two powers – Britain and Egypt in the case of Sudan, and Britain and France in the case of New Hebrides.[7]

With respect to the main goal of the chapter, we must emphasize how unique the protectorate's administration as built on the idea of sharing competences between Britain and local political elites. While the British administration made a strategic decision about (1) foreign policy of each protectorate (foreign policy must have followed the main vision of Britain), (2) type of education and health care system, and (3) level of taxes and fees, African elites could follow their own domestic policies. African authorities made decisions about management of home affairs including administration of kingship or keeping daily habits.[8]

British interest in Africa must be seen in wider context of that era. During the first half of nineteenth century, Africa remained a continent where "hic sunt leones" in many ways, and only coastal areas were colonized due to their high relevancy for slave trade. Slave trade, partly based on cooperation with local African elites, did not force European traders to penetrate to the inland of Africa, and for many of decades the European activities were situated only close to the sea harbor. This situation changed dramatically in the last third of nineteenth century when newly established European powers (German, Italy, and Belgium) started to have colonial aspirations. The era of Scramble for Africa entered to its final stage immediately after the Berlin Conference of 1884–1885. The principle of effective occupation became the crucial outcome of the meeting and the spheres of influences were designated.[9]

After having signed the concluding memorandum Britain, started to fulfill its ambition to interconnect North/Egypt and South/Cape Town of the continent and, in words of Cecil Rhodes, create an empire "from North to South" with southern Africa (namely Bechuanaland) as a Suez of British Africa.[10] British colonial policy has been characterized by "indirect rule," relying on cooperation between a pretty small number of colonial officers, and employment of a huge number of local politics and elites.[11] British concentrated on foreign policy accompanied by spreading of English and Christianity. Systems of Christian missions headed by London Missionary Society brought to Africa diametrically new habits and rules, which have strongly affected African societies until nowadays. The idea of Christianity and its proselytization must be seen in the context of the British civilizing mission at all British overseas steps. According to this idea, Britain stood at the top of development of mankind with the duty to show the rest of non-civilized world how to development itself. The White Man's Burden (in the words of Rudyard Kipling) as an integral part of British activities during the nineteenth century represented the cornerstone of British policy, especially towards Africa. Beside the Union of South Africa, African colonies were seen as non-developed areas and Britain sought to look after them. This duty, strongly embedded in British society, was not weakened until the 1950s, when the international order changed dramatically and wind of changes blew through the continent.[12]

Dissemination of British values and principles was an integral part of British endeavors. One can claim – with just a little exaggeration – that apart from polo playgrounds, the Britons built roads and railways, connecting the key hubs of their Empire. It is therefore no wonder that, for instance, the African South has the densest railway network on the continent. Together with the material characteristics of the British Empire, principles of liberalism and free trade were spread by means of British colonialism, which had been basically founded on both. Activities of trading companies were typical for that era; their foundation was essentially linked with the culture of the British Isles. The companies were sort of joint stock enterprises, whose aim was to maximize profit, exploiting the most attractive geographical areas for the purpose. The trading companies were the real flagships of English colonial power. Headed by capable entrepreneurs motivated by money, these businesses entered previously unknown territories, where they controlled trade with any major local commodity. As fate would have it, at the time when Scramble for Africa culminated, there were huge deposits of gold and diamonds discovered in the south, opening space for new business ventures in this part of Africa.

Southern Africa and British interests

New mineral resources made British citizens interested in this part of the planet, about which they had had only a sketchy notion. Suddenly, British presence appeared not just of some civilizing importance, but also as a contributing force of growth of the British economy, driven by the successes of the Industrial Revolution, unrivalled in the then world. Cecil Rhodes became the figurehead; as a not very healthy young man he had left Britain to look for a better future in south Africa. It did not take him long to found the British South African Company (BSAC), taking commercial and political control of what is today called Zambia, Zimbabwe, and Malawi, and within a short period of time these three countries were made in fact into private properties of Cecil Rhodes.[13] However, his ambitions were not limited to business – he was a skilled politician, committed to the vision of unified British domains in Africa – from Egypt all the way to Cape Town. Rhodes was deeply convinced that British colonialism made sense, and that it was necessary to use all means available to prevent the British Empire from losing a single territory. Along these lines he even urged to re-join the United States of America to the Crown – a hundred years after they had declared independence. It is only logical that Rhodes contemplated where to direct his next efforts, focusing his attention on Bechuanaland. In other words:

consolidation of positions could not materialize without the annexation of Bechuanaland, because this vast region was naturally linked to both southern Africa and the neighboring "Rhodes lands." The main point was its vast area with very few people. Most of the territory was covered by Kalahari Desert, which made an impression on Rhodes that it would be no big deal to annex it. However, it should be noted that Rhodes's activities were his private affairs, and he did not act in the name of Britain as a whole. His actions were thoroughly unilateral – he believed the British would appreciate them adequately, as he was led by his free spirit and strong belief in free market.

The activities in the central part of southern Africa should be considered in a wider geopolitical context, linked to the colonial activities of other European powers. Germans deserve to be mentioned first, being more assertive as a result of their joining the colonial competition later. Occupation of German southwest Africa was just the first step on the road to achieving a larger German vision, which was to connect the southwest with the German eastern Africa (or Tanganyika). This bold plan collided with the aforementioned British interests in southern Africa.[14] The ascend of Germany into European colonial politics is associated with the era following immediately after the German unification, yet despite its belatedness, it has, in some cases, witnessed a more dramatic course of events. The possession of a colonial empire represented a significant feature of great-power politics in the nineteenth century, and so a newly united Germany aspired to gain non-European territories. From the British perspective, the German colonial ambitions that mattered the most were the ones which were initiated shortly after the unification of the country and culminated during the Berlin Conference in 1884–1885 that testified Germany's entry onto the stage of colonial powers. In a quick session Germany thus gained control over Southwest Africa, German East Africa, Togo, and Cameroon.[15] Given that Germany entered its colonial stage among the latest contenders, it was bound to come across the presence of other European powers, most notably Britain, which was present in regions directly bordering the German territories.[16] This apparent British-German antagonism manifested in the region of south Africa. The first piece of evidence documenting the mutual clashes of interests revolves around the creation of the Caprivi Strip that runs inward from the territory of southwest Africa to the Zambezi River and follows the northern border of Bechuanaland. Yet Germans paid due attention to the region of Boer provinces Transvaal and the Orange Free State into which, according to numerous German representatives, German migration meant to bolster the non-British segment of South-African society was supposed to be headed. Traditionally, the Boers were perceived as close allies of Germans and so through mutual cooperation Germans were bent on weakening the position of the British in the region. Driven by the discovery of gold in

Transvaal in 1886, which significantly increased the economic potential of the region, Germans moving in to the provinces during the 1890s were able to put that to a good use. The growing number of German-speaking residents was supposed to be accompanied by the construction of a railroad connecting both regions with the coast so as to, eventually, expand Germany's influence in the entire region. Santa Lucia Bay represented a pivotal region alongside the Indian Ocean. Historically speaking, this territory had been controlled by the Zulus whose king granted Germans a concession for 60 acres of land meant for constructing the railroad all the way to Transvaal in 1884. Its immediate vicinity was supposed to witness the erection of dwellings for German immigrants.[17] British response did not take long and as a consequence the hopes of strengthening the alliance between Germans and Zulus were quashed and thus this German vision remained unfulfilled. Nevertheless, German activities did not cease and made the British well realize the potentially growing influence of Germany. As such, Britain turned its attention to Bechuanaland; a key territory that was meant to play the role of a buffer between southwest Africa and Transvaal.

A major influence of the British behavior in the region was, as already mentioned, the Boer element. The origin of Boers can be found among religious refugees fleeing Europe for southern Africa, looking for a new life in this part of the world. Their perception of their own identity was based on the idea that South Africa was their homeland, meaning they had an undisputed claim to the country. The situation got rather complicated when the British arrived; they had a number of specific features when compared to the Boers. Different worldview was derived from the religion. The Boers were Calvinists, seeing themselves as God's chosen people, while the British Protestants encouraged freedom of thought and trade, and after the slave trade was prohibited, they could not continue enslavement of the natives any longer. As opposed to the Boers, who were not able to comprehend why they should not use the locals for menial jobs, when the locals simply did not possess the same qualities. The conflict got so serious that the Boers started withdrawing inlands. During their famous Great Trek, they clashed with a number of local tribes whom they defeated, and when the Brits pushed them out of Cape Town, they settled further from the ocean and created Transvaal and the Orange Free State. Beside the two Boer republics, there were two British states, and the Anglo-Boer wars started between them at the end of the nineteenth century.[18] The conflict affected not just the south African territory, but also the three lands bravely refuting to join any of the Boer republics, which, in turn, tried to change this repeatedly.

The wider geopolitical context was clear in relations between the British and the Boers. These two segments vied for consolidation of their positions; it was surprising for the British to what extent and how intensely the Boers were able to develop their own political concepts of regional administration. At the same time, the British had their particular regional interests they wanted to protect at the lowest possible costs. A pragmatic agreement with local elites was therefore selected as a convenient method of achieving this. While the Boers led by the Transvaal president Paul Kruger wished to create a great white Boer South Africa, Rhodes, controlling BSCA, called for a Great British Empire instead, and the British imperial establishment itself apparently had no idea for which strategy to follow. It was Rhodes in particular who decisively responded to the growing German-Transvaal partnership by accelerating the establishment of a protectorate over Bechuanaland that lay west of Transvaal. Similarly, he decided to take control over the regions of Mashonoland and Matabeleland (today's Zimbabwe). All Rhodes' steps were headed toward a single goal of establishing a large British South Africa reaching from Cape Town to the areas surrounding the Zambezi River.[19]

A crucial event for buttressing the British governance in South Africa occurred with the creation of the Office of High Commissioner in the year 1846 that aimed at protecting British interests in the region. Between 1847 and 1900 (with the exception of the period 1879–1881) the office was headed by a person titled the Cape Colony governor.[20] Once The South-African Union was established as a dominion, he held, at the same time, the position of the General Governor of this region too. The one titled the High Commissioner was chairing an office called the South African High Commission, the task of which lay in administrating the protectorates of Basutoland, Bechuanaland, and Swaziland. Each of these protectorates was then governed by a local resident commissioner who answered to the South African High Commission. After 1931, when the South-African Union gained independence, the positions of the General Governor and High Commissioner were separated.[21]

The British presence in Africa was typified by the above-mentioned principle of indirect rule, which in the case of the three south African territories took on a standalone form to the extent that it became referred to and recognized as parallel rule. In comparison to indirect rule incorporating traditional structures into the British governance so meticulously that these participated in creating the rules and the code of conduct for the British administration – which was the standard modus operandi in the remainder of British Africa – parallel rule saw two systems de facto existing next to each other.[22]

Bechuanaland protectorate

Bechuanaland was for a long time a territory nobody had shown any interest in, being a sparsely populated desert, offering pretty little at the first sight. The area was not even a target of so-called economic colonialism – in which European businessmen made concession contracts with the locals that allowed them to exercise control over trade in certain region. As Bechuanaland was quite unattractive in this respect, the businessmen turned their attention elsewhere. The situation changed dramatically in relation to the Scramble for Africa, which made Bechuanaland an area of strategic importance.[23]

Low number of inhabitants, of whom most lived as hunters and gatherers, had a negative impact on the perception of Bechuanaland by its neighbors. This meant the area was seen as a no-man's land, where there was free entry for everybody – and the Boers used the opportunity in the early 1880s. At that time two Boer republics were not sufficient anymore, and other small Boer states were established regardless of the South African borders. Thus Stellaland republic and Goshen state emerged in the 1880s, located at the border with the Protectorate (or – more specifically – encroaching on its territory). Both these republics were shortly re-incorporated into the areas under British control, yet the population in Bechuanaland had to face the fundamental question: how to react to the ever-growing Boer ambitions?[24]

Relations between the British and the Boers were tense – this was related to the assertiveness with which the Boers approached negotiations. Mutual animosity was on the rise, and this made life difficult for the African indigenous population, forced to choose whether they would defend their independence until possible (or better to say very likely) defeat, while the Battle of Blood River (where Zulu troop were routed) remained a bitter memory in their minds. The rout of the impressive Zulu army was a memento for all the natives, should they even play with the idea of rebellion against the Boers; they did everything they could not to be subdued to the Boer rule. Political representation of Bechuanaland had to make a major decision: to continue resistance to the Boer expansionist attempts and to hope for their failure, or to try to face alone the Boer armed units and be sure of a rout, or to ask for help from the strong player, who would ensure their security in exchange for certain concessions.

The third possibility seemed to be the best, providing a chance for a Bechuanaland without the Boer influence and at least a certain level of autonomy for local political representation. Tswana people under their leader Khama III reached this conclusion and came to London in the early 1880s to negotiate the parameters of cooperation with the British. Before we get to the London talks, we should say a few words about King Khama III, who – with hindsight – made a bold step and maintained independence, and in a way contributed to the declaration of independent Botswana 80 years later. Khama III was one of the first locals who "manifested" the influence of European missions. He accepted baptism in the mid-1880s from a German Lutheran priest, but later banned the Lutherans and became ardent follower of London Missionary Society.[25] Khama III was among the first members of his tribe to do that, soon to be followed by others. After he married a Christian, his previously completely marginal area was to develop into a major component of the British Empire.

The London talks in the presence of three ruling Tswana kings (Bothoen I, Sebele I, and Khama III), accompanied by two missionaries (Edwin Lloyd, William C. Wolloughby) were viewed with utmost suspicion by the British officials.[26] British representative Chamberlain could not grasp why he was to be cooperating in any way with the Tswanas, initially proposing they should settle the matters themselves, in agreement with the Rhodes's company. British administration planned to cooperate with BSAC in the issue of governing Bechuanaland, not paying much attention. However, the Tswanas insisted and refused to leave Britain after the first failed round of talks. In the meantime they successfully approached the British public that was not deaf to their grievances, and thanks to the public support a new round of meetings took place. Agreement was finally reached that Bechuanaland would be a British protectorate, and a new railway was to be built through its territory from the neighboring Rhodesia.[27] It was this railway that played a major role during the Anglo-Boer Wars, because it transported soldiers of the British Empire to fight the Boers. Ordinary people of Bechuanaland were determined to guard the border between the Protectorate and south African provinces, making sure no Boer units entered their homeland secretly. Thus the Brits took control over Bechuanaland in 1885. Shortly after the London talks were concluded the British side decided to reorganize the Protectorate, joining its southern part with the then south African province of Cape Colony. The capital Mafikeng was outside Bechuanaland, which resulted in a paradox: the center of administrative territory was not located within the boundaries. Mafikeng performed the function of capital city from 1895 until declaration of independence of Botswana in the 1960s.[28]

Even though there were no known natural resources in the territory of Bechuanaland at the time of the birth of the protectorate (diamonds were discovered several years after the declaration of independence), the whole area bore much significance given its geopolitical potential that the British were well aware of. Bechuanaland served as a territory separating German Southwest Africa from Boorish Transvaal. Therefore, Britain, realizing the growing influence of the German-Boorish partnership, sought to respond to the emerging alliance of its rivals by expanding its empire so as to secure the area known as the Suez of South Africa.[29] The region of Bechuanaland heightened its importance after its southern part witnessed the construction of a railroad connecting British Cape Town with regions in Central Africa under the control of Rhodes' BSAC.

As mentioned, a prominent feature of British presence in Bechuanaland lies in the so-called parallel rule, or dual rule, which stemmed from a conviction that Bechuanaland did not require any form of direct administration and that the only required ingredient of the region would be its external security. Constant pressure mounted by the Boers and Germans alike made Khama III ask for protection, and the British disinterest in the internal administration of the region left domestic affairs within the hands of the locals.[30] The region of Bechuanaland consisted of three types – areas inhabited exclusively by Africans governed by the locals, areas populated by Europeans whose affairs were managed by the British governance abiding by the principles of the Roman-Dutch legal system, and areas known as the tracts of Crown land.[31] A pivotal traditional institution that the Britons kept intact, and respected, was *kgotla*, which embodied a kind of community council that granted every free man the right to speak out. Based on a discussion and after reaching a joint consensus, decisions that the locals upheld were reached and accepted. Although it may seem as if the British governance was virtually ideal, it was not devoid of some undeniable drawbacks either. The fact that the British demonstrated little to no interest in the protectorate, and basically refrained from committing any means into the social or economic development of the region, posed a major limitation. This was caused by the absence of any notable natural resources across the region at that time and so the sole importance of this territory rested on its location only. Yet also, the British knew the risks of leaving the internal development of a region unsupervised and thus strengthened the competences of the High Commissioner from 1891 onwards, who was able to dismiss the tribe leader (kgosi) for insubordination.[32]

Swaziland protectorate

While Bechuanaland was a huge chunk of land with tremendous strategic importance, little Swaziland wedged between the Portuguese interests in Mozambique and British ambitions in South Africa was considered a marginal area. Portuguese attempts at joining the little kingdom were connected with the so-called pink map that counted on a daring plan to combine Portuguese domains Angola and Mozambique, including Swaziland. The idea finally did not take root, but other neighbors became interested in Swaziland, namely the Boers, already established in the South African space. Boer interest in Swaziland was closely linked to the fact that vast deposits of gold and diamonds were found in the territory of today's republic of South Africa in the last third of the nineteenth century – relatively close to the borders with Swaziland. The representatives of Boorish Transvaal endeavored to expand their territory into the region of Delagoa Bay possessed by the Portuguese, yet such intention repeatedly failed to materialize. A pivotal milestone for maintaining the independence of Swaziland came to pass with the Pretoria Convention in 1881, which acknowledged that the territory of Swaziland will not be ceded to any other political entity, and thus made room for negotiations between the British government and the representatives of the kingdom about the form of cooperation.[33]

Back then there was considerable Euro-African community in Swaziland that emerged as a result of relations usually between white men and local black women.[34] The white men came to Swaziland because of the concession award policy that represented a substantial aspect of local life in the second half of the nineteenth century. The king of Swaziland had the right to grant concessions to mine minerals, or to do business in various fields, in exchange for taxes paid to him. New gold veins had been found recently, and the resulting gold rush in neighboring Transvaal province attracted many adventurers to Swaziland, where they applied for concessions.[35] Caucasians from all parts of the world were coming here; the Brits and Boers were joined for example by interested Australians. Many Boers subsequently lived in the areas near the border between Transvaal and Swaziland, while a small area between both the regions was rather symptomatically named Small Free State. Even though the existence of this small administrative unit could seem a negligible episode, it was not. The Boers showed readiness for serious penetration into Swaziland territory, and it was clear that to keep independence would be extremely difficult. Boer racism provoked anxiety of local population due to fears of losing their identity, and similarly to Bechuanaland case representatives of Swaziland started negotiations with British government about terms of protection.[36]

British willingness to be involved in the protection of a small African kingdom shall be seen in a wider geopolitical context of South Africa at the end of the nineteenth century. The period witnessed growing tensions between the British and the Boers, which finally led to outburst of Anglo-Boer wars, whose sole point was to settle the issue of spheres of influence. Boers controlled Transvaal and Orange Free State, and strove to extend their power through the Cape Colony and Natal – controlled by the British. During the first Anglo-Boer War, Swaziland was occupied by the British for the first time, while its conclusion (1902) saw the British government appoint a special commissary tasked with governing the territory. One of the first issues that the British administration had to tackle was the question of land distribution among the locals and newly arriving white settlers. Whereas the settlers claimed that they purchased the land and thus had the right to do as they see fit with it, the representatives of Swaziland countered that they granted the land to the settlers. Eventually, the British administration established a special commission dedicated to solving territorial disputes between white colonists and local inhabitants. Finally, it delineated the spheres of influence for white settlers and local residents much to the repeated disapproval of the representatives of Swaziland. The period of British governance was, to a large extent, epitomized by solving territorial issues.[37]

The Anglo-Boer conflict claimed thousands of lives and obviously affected the neighboring regions. Swaziland representatives were anxious about Boer expansionism, and preferred protection provided by the British, even at the cost of losing their independence. In the last decade of the nineteenth century a series of the so-called conventions were signed, gradually curtailing the independence. The process of incorporation of Swaziland into the British Empire was completed by 1906, when the country officially became British Protectorate.[38]

Basutoland

From a European viewpoint, Basutoland started to attract some attention only in the nineteenth century, when basic characteristics of future modern Lesotho were formed. The political central figure responsible for initiation of modernization process of traditional Basotho society was Moshoeshoe, known since the 1830s as Morena e Moholo. As a leader of Sotho tribes he centralized his power, and step by step consolidated his authority, which he expanded from the capital Thaba Bosiu. The situation in the little mountainous kingdom was relatively calm, until external factors intervened in the form of Boer farmers and European missionaries and adventurers attracted to Drakensberg area. Even though Moshoeshoe and his subjects looked at the businessmen, swashbucklers, and holy men with mistrust, the Boers proved to be the greatest threat, as they were searching for a new land to settle. Loyal Moshoeshoe's allies were members of Paris Evangelical Mission Society, and with their help he succeeded to repel the ever-increasing ambitions of Caucasian population of south Africa.[39] Despite this support, arable fields were more and more occupied by white settlers, who finally drove the original peoples of Basutoland inland.[40]

As in the cases of Bechuanaland and Swaziland, the British played a key role in the development of Basutoland; as early as in 1868 they made it part of the regions administered by the High Commissioner for South Africa. After three years under the High Commissioner for South Africa, the representation of Cape Colony tried to annex Basutoland, but the rule was not popular, and a short time later it was replaced by the British again. Similar to the above-mentioned two cases, the scenario was better than annexation by the Boers, and Basutoland accepted the British presence. The development of this small rural kingdom was, to a great extent, affected by the discovery of diamonds. Like in Swaziland, thanks to the diamond and gold rushes, technical innovations were spreading in Basutoland, contributing to its modernization. Influx of money from mine workers resulted in major changes to the local society in the last third of the nineteenth century, accompanied by population growth, improved access to health care, and overall increase of wealth.[41] After the Cape Colony excess Basutoland became Protectorate within the British imperial system, and its administration was exclusively British. The significance of Basutoland lay, inter alia, in its important strategic location. In spite of being a landlocked territory, it was located along the road between the coast and the inland; the Orange River flowed through here and it directly neighbored the Orange Free State. The representatives of the Boorish provinces strove to expand their region by annexing Basutoland, which, they believed, would result in weakening the British position due to considerably aggravating their means of communication between the coastal provinces of Cape and Natal.[42]

Akin to Bechuanaland, the case of Basutoland merits invoking the existence of parallel rule, i.e. the concomitant functioning of British and local structures. During the first half of the twentieth century Basutoland became a territory de facto dependent on its surrounding and unable to function by itself. Whereas, historically speaking, Basutoland used to meet the food consumption of its citizens by utilizing its own sources; throughout the first third of the twentieth century, it was turned into a pure importer of all basic kinds of food. In tandem with large swaths of workers laboring outside the boundaries of the protectorate, it conveyed an unmistaken dependence on the outside world.

Administration of British domains

The Anglo-Boer wars ended in 1902 by a treaty claiming that the British had won the war, but at the same time they had lost the peace. This means that the British may have protected their lands against continued Boer expansion, and the Boers finally had to surrender, but the power arrangements based on the signed treaty indicated that the Boers would become politically stronger element. Once the war was over, the issue of territorial alignment of the south African region re-entered the spotlight. The representatives of Boorish Transvaal, albeit being defeated in the war, did not do away with ambitions regarding territorial expansion and demanded territorial adjustments. Their gaze was fixed upon two particular areas – Mozambique and Swaziland.[43] The issue of annexing Swaziland had already been tabled several times before, with its chief proponent being the Prime Minister Botha of the Transvaal province.[44]

This post-war era was marked by discussions about further territorial adjustments to the South-African region, with the Selborne Memorandum being one of the documents attempting to outline a possible way of doing so by accommodating and adopting "national expansion." This, following the example of the United States or Canada, was meant to expand and unite the existing south African regions into one political entity governed by white inhabitants. The question of the future development of South Africa thus stood at a precipice – to declare independence as a republic or to seek inspiration in other territories of the British Empire and become a dominion?[45] Union of South Africa was established in 1910 with dominion status, and Britain was less and less able to intervene in its development. The Union of South Africa made it no secret that its main goal was to create "Great South Africa" to include also Bechuanaland, Swaziland, and Basutoland, and in ideal case also Rhodesia and Nyasaland.

The three regions were administered as High Commissioner Territories, whereas the office was founded in 1910, after the Union of South Africa got independence. Until 1924, the office (together with the administration of the Union of South Africa and Southern Rhodesia) was subordinated to the Colonial Office in London, gradually transformed into the Commonwealth Relations Office. So-called Proclamations were issued for each of the territories, under the responsibility of the High Commissioner, whose authority was derived from the Foreign Jurisdiction Act of 1890 and its Order-in-Council of 1891. Individual Proclamations were the implemented by resident commissioners in charge of individual protectorates.[46]

The three territories watched the creation of the Union of South Africa with disapproval, because they were, rightfully so, afraid of a new political unit trying to annex them, practically ending their existence. It was a certain advantage that Basutoland was not largely inhabited by white population, and the administration remained in the locals' hands. The other two territories were preserved for similar reasons. It was namely the people in Bechuanaland who pointed out problems arising in relation to the indigenous segment in the neighboring German southwestern Africa, where genocide of Herers took place in the early twentieth century; Bechuanaland was afraid what would happen, should the Boers prevail in the region, strongly supporting the Germans.[47]

The British administration worked on the parallel rule principle throughout the first half of the twentieth century, until the three territories took roads to independence. The British administration was financed by taxes collected in the territories, while more money was leaving the area than was brought in. Despite numerous problems thanks to the British presence, the three countries could begin their independent efforts in the 1960s. Initially, Britain deemed that the trio of these countries would be unable to reach full-scale independence and, especially in the case of Basutoland and Swaziland, was convinced that some form of dependence on the British government would be maintained. Supposedly, a small number of inhabitants indicated that these countries would be short of human resources to be governed independently, and the proximity of the Republic of South Africa magnified the threat of being incorporated into a state of apartheid. Furthermore, this trio of countries was notably reliant on the South African economy and provided large portions of their productive populaces for South African mines. Nevertheless, annexation by the Republic of South Africa failed to materialize also due to the race-driven regime gradually retreating into international isolation, which rendered expanding its territory by annexing new regions unacceptable.

Basutoland became independent in 1966 as Lesotho, and Bechuanaland as Botswana, followed in 1968 by Swaziland; in all three cases series of negotiations preceded the act of declaration, the aim of which was to prepare for the new status. The negotiations included discussions of political setup in the new-born independent countries, accompanied by the first constitutional texts adopted in their histories.

Elections were organized in Bechuanaland in 1965 – after negotiations on the constitution. As was the custom in Westminster, Great Britain came up with the idea of bicameral parliament and position of prime minister, taken by Seretse Khama after the elections. He later became president, and for many years to come the most influential politician, leading the country towards political and economic stability.[48] Negotiations in Lesotho followed a similar pattern, but soon after the declaration of independence, the regime changed with Chief Jonathan, who kept the country in state of emergency for 16 years, and abolished monarchy until 1986.[49] The same applied to Swaziland's negotiations about the new political system before independence, culminating in the adoption of the first constitution in 1967. Even though the British had an ambition to introduce Westminster model of government in Swaziland, its principles did not take root there, and the country went its absolutist way.[50]

Conclusion

The purpose of this text was to present the character of the British colonial rule in three marginal areas of South Africa; and while it is clear that Swaziland, Bechuanaland, and Basutoland were not frequent topics of discussions in the British Empire, their importance was not to be underestimated given their strategic locations. Bechuanaland as the gateway to African inland and bridge of British interests in the north and south of the continent was a region that attracted major attention of all the neighboring powers. The railroad connecting southern Rhodesia and South African provinces was of major importance, working as transportation artery, allowing the British to perform their rule. Considering the minimum level of population, which is concentrated almost exclusively in the south-eastern part of the country, its existence was pivotal for Britain. The Administration of Swaziland and Basutoland was an opportunity for the British to weaken the position of Afrikaans, as their political influence was growing steadily from 1910, and after the apartheid policy was officially declared in 1948, it became apparent that British presence gave the two kingdoms hope for independence. The specific feature of British rule in the three territories was its format. The representatives of all three regions invited the British and asked to be incorporated into the British colonial system, and there was quite a symbiotic relationship between local elites and British officials, resulting in a calm process of power transition in the 1960s. While Botswana headed for stability, the remaining two have experienced a much more complicated political development, but no one can blame Britain for that – the culprits are local political elites.

Notes

1 Gretchen Bauer and Scott D. Taylor, *Politics in Southern Africa: State and Society in Transition* (London: Lynne Rienner Publishers, 2005), 86.
2 Matthew Lange, James Mahoney, and Matthias von Hau, "Colonialism and Development: A Comparative Analysis of Spanish and British Colonies," *American Journal of Sociology*, 111: 5 (2006), 1427; Joseph Chamberlain, "The True Conception of Empire," in: *The Worlds Famous Orations*, Vol. V (1897).
3 Martin Pugh, *Britain Since 1789: A Concise History* (Hampshire: Macmillan Press, 1999), 83.
4 After the occupation of Aden, Britain gained a new alternative route to India.
5 See e.g. Robert Johnson, *British Imperialism* (New York: Palgrave Macmillan, 2003) to learn more about the individual stages of British colonialism.
6 M. Epstein (ed.), *The Statesman's Year-Book: Statistical and Historical Annual of the States of the World for the Year 1928* (London: Macmillan and Co., 1928), 75.
7 For more information about New Hebrides, see David W. McIntyre, *Winding Up the British Empire in the Pacific Islands* (Oxford: Oxford University Press, 2014). For more information about Sudan, see M. W. Daly, *Imperial Sudan: The Anglo-Egyptian Condominium 1934–1956* (Cambridge: Cambridge University Press, 1991).
8 It was fairly common that the status of the individual territories within the British Empire kept changing over the years and apart from the trio of Bechuanaland, Basutoland, and Swaziland, other regions in Africa also held the status of a protectorate at some point. For a complex overview, see e.g. Michael Havinden and David Meredith, *Colonialism and Development: Britain and Its Tropical Colonies 1850–1960* (London: Routledge, 1993), 71–73.
9 M. E. Chamberlain, *The Scramble for Africa* (London: Routledge, 2013), 53–54; James R. Lehning, *European Colonialism Since 1700* (New York: Cambridge University Press, 2013), 186.
10 Henryk Zins, "The International Context of the Creation of the Bechuanaland Protectorate in 1885," *PULA Journal of African Studies*, 11: 1 (1997), 54.

11 Gretchen Bauer and Scott D. Taylor, *Politics in Southern Africa: State and Society in Transition* (London: Lynne Rienner Publishers, 2005), 86.
12 Michael Mann, "'Torchbearers Upon the Path of Progress'. Britain's Ideology of a Moral and Material Progress in India. An Introductory Essay," in: *Colonialism as Civilizing Mission: Cultural Ideology in British India*, ed. by H. Fischer-Tiné and M. Mann (London: Wimbledon Publishing Company, 2004), 2.
13 Neil Parsons, *King Khama Emperor Joe and the Great White Queen Victorian Britain Through African Eyes* (Chicago: The University of Chicago Press, 1982), 24.
14 Relations between Southwest Africa, later Namibia and current Botswana, were in fact solved only in the early 1990s, when dispute over an island on Chobe River was settled. The island was finally joined with Botswana. Another major issue complicating mutual relations was Namibia's plan to build water supply pipeline through Caprivi Strip (Zambezi region) all the way to Okavango River, and pump water from there. This plan failed, too.
15 S. Friedrichsmeyer, S. Lennox, and S. Zantop (eds.), *The Imperialism Imagination: German Colonialism and Its Legacy* (Ann Arbor: University of Michigan Press, 1998), 9–10.
16 Every European power exercised its own specific colonial policy with notably differing results. Stating that: "The English, which consists in raking colonies with colonists; the German, which collects colonists without colonies; and the French, which sets up colonies without colonists" captures the essence of the colonial activities of three essential European powers of the last third of the nineteenth century. D. N. Pyeatt, *Heligoland and the Making of the Anglo-German Colonial Agreement in 1890: A Thesis in History* (Lubbock: Texas Tech University, 1998), 13.
17 C. D. Penner, "Germany and the Transvaal Before 1896," *Journal of Modern History*, 12: 1 (1940), 32–33.
18 Martin Meredith, *Diamonds, Gold and War: The British, the Boers, and the Making of South Africa* (New York: Simon & Schuster, 2008), 82.
19 P. J. Cain and A. G. Hopkins, *British Imperialism 1688–2015* (Oxon: Routledge, 2016), 347.
20 Neil Parsons, *King Khama Emperor Joe and the Great White Queen: Victorian Britain through African Eyes* (Chicago: University of Chicago Press, 1998), 34.
21 James Olson and Robert Shadle (eds.), *Historical Dictionary of the British Empire* (Westport: Greenwood Press, 1996), 1037.
22 Harol M. Glass, *South African Policy Towards Basutoland* (Johannesburg: The South African Institute of International Affairs, 1966), 11.
23 Daron Acemoglu, Simon Johnson and James A. Robinson, "An African Success Story: Botswana," in: *Search of Prosperity: Analytic Narratives on Economic Growth*, ed. by Dani Rodrik (Princeton: Princeton University Press, 2003), 13.
24 A. Walker (ed.), *The Cambridge History of the British Empire: Vol. VIII. South Africa, Rhodesia, and the High Commission Territories* (New York: Cambridge University Press, 1963), 519.
25 Roland Oliver and G. N. Sanderson (eds.), *The Cambridge History of Africa: Volume 6. From 1870 to 1905* (Cambridge: Cambridge University Press, 1985), 405; Niall Ferguson, *Empire: How Britain Made the Modern World* (London: Penguin Books, 2004), 123–133.
26 Fred Morton, Jeff Ramsay, and Part T. Mgadla, *Historical Dictionary of Botswana* (Lanham: Scarecrow Press, 2008), 9.

27 The railway was actually built, and led, from South Rhodesian Bulawayo via eastern headland of Bechuanaland, Francistown, and Lobatse, all the way to the Union of South Africa. Neil Parsons, *King Khama Emperor Joe and the Great White Queen: Victorian Britain Through African Eyes* (Chicago: University of Chicago Press, 1998), 33.

28 Vryburg was the capital between 1885 and 1895.

29 Ronald Hyam, *The Failure of South African Expansion 1908–1948* (London: Palgrave Macmillan Press, 1972), 12–13.

30 Deborah A. Schmitt, *The Bechuanaland Pionners and Gunners* (Westport: Praeger Publishers, 2006), 43.

31 Kamran A. Afzal and Mark Considine, *Democratic Accountability and International Human Development: Regimes, Institutions and Resources* (Oxon: Routledge, 2015), 144.

32 Ibid., 144.

33 E. A. Walker and L. Harlech, "The British South African Territories," *African Affairs*, 44: 175 (1945), 64.

34 Alan R. Booth, *Historical Dictionary of Swaziland*, 2nd Edition (Lanham: Scarecrow Press, 2000), 27, 104, 114.

35 Hugh Gillis, *The Kingdom of Swaziland: Studies in Political History* (Westport: Greenwood Press, 1999), 51–55; Christian Potholm, *Swaziland: The Dynamics of Political Modernization* (Berkeley: University of California Press, 1993), 53.

36 Rita Byrnes (ed.), *South Africa: A Country Study* (USA: PO for the Library of Congress, 1996), unpaged.

37 Petros Qambukusa Magagula, *Swaziland's Relations With Britain and South Africa Since 1968, Durham Theses* (Durham: Durham University, 1998), 15–19.

38 F. J. Mashasha, *The Swazi and Land Partition (1902–1910)*. Collected Seminar Papers. Institute of Commonwealth Studies, 17 (1974), 88.

39 The support of Paris Evangelical Mission Society was motivated by the simple fact that the French saw the Brits as their competitors, and it was only natural for them to stand behind any activity aimed at curtailing the British influence.

40 Scott Rosenberg and Richard F. Weisfelder, *Historical Dictionary of Lesotho* (Lanham: Scarecrow Press, 2013), 5–6.

41 Elizabeth A. Eldredge, *A South African Kingdom: The Pursuit of Security in Nineteenth-Century Lesotho* (New York: Cambridge University Press, 2002), 11.

42 E. A. Walker and L. Harlech, "The British South African Territories," *African Affairs*, 44: 175 (1945), 63.

43 Rhodes, seeking the annexation of regions adjacent to Port Beira, too, showed interest in Mozambique by the end of the nineteenth century. Yet his bid failed, because the mutual British-Portuguese relations were addressed by a treaty from 1891 that confined the Portuguese sphere of influence on the Eastern coast. Ronald Hyam, *The Failure of South African Expansion 1908–1948* (London: Palgrave Macmillan Press, 1972), 14.

44 Ronald Hyam, *The Failure of South African Expansion 1908–1948* (London: Palgrave Macmillan Press, 1972), 25.

45 Stanely Trapido and Ian Phimister, "Imperialism, Settler Identities and Colonial Capitalism: The Hundred Year Origins of the 1899 South African War," *Historia*, 53: 1 (2008), 71.

46 Fred Morton, Jeff Ramsay, and Part T. Mgadla, *Historical Dictionary of Botswana* (Lanham: Scarecrow Press, 2008), 136–137.

47 For more information about Herero genocide see Jeremy Sarkin, *Germany's Genocide of the Herero: Kaiser Wilhelm II, His General, His Settlers, His Soldiers* (Cape Town: UCT Press, 2011).

48 Gretchen Bauer and Scott D. Taylor, *Politics in Southern Africa: State and Society in Transition* (London: Lynne Rienner Publishers, 2005), 87.

49 Scott Rosenberg and Richard F. Weisfelder, *Historical Dictionary of Lesotho* (Lahman: Scarecrow Press, 2013), 10.

50 J. H. Proctor, "Traditionalism and Parliamentary Government in Swaziland," *African Affairs*, 72: 288 (1973), 274.

Bibliography

Abbink, Jon (1998) "An Historical-Anthropological Approach to Islam in Ethiopia: Issues of Identity and Politics." *Journal of African Cultural Studies*, 11 (2), 109–124.

Abbink, Jon (2011) "Religion in Public Spaces: Emerging Muslim-Christian Polemics in Ethiopia." *African Affairs*, 110 (439), 253–274.

Abdallah, Abdo A. (2008) "State Building, Independence and Post-Conflict Reconstruction in Djibouti." In: *Post-Conflict Peace-Building in the Horn of Africa*, ed. by Ulf Johansson Dahre. Lund: Lund University, 275–276.

Abir, Mordechai (1980) "The Emergence and Consolidation of the Monarchies of Enarea and Jimma in the First Half of the Nineteenth Century." *Journal of African History*, 6 (2), 205–219.

Abir, Mordechai (1980) *Ethiopia and the Red Sea: The Rise and Decline of the Solomonic Dynasty and Muslim-European Rivalry in the Region*. London: Frank Cass and Company.

Acemoglu, Daron, Simon Johnson, and James A. Robinson (2003) "An African Success Story: Botswana." In: *Search of Prosperity: Analytic Narratives on Economic Growth*, ed. by Dani Rodrik. Princeton: Princeton University Press, 80–119.

Afzal, Kamran A. and Mark Considine (2015) *Democratic Accountability and International Human Development: Regimes, Institutions and Resources*. Oxon: Routledge.

Ahmed, Ismail I. and Reginald Herbold Green (1999) "The Heritage of War and State Collapse in Somalia and Somaliland: Local-level Effects, External Interventions and Reconstruction." *Third World Quarterly*, 20 (1), 113–127.

Asrat, M. (2003) *Modernity and Change in Ethiopia: 1941–1991. From Feudalism to Ethnic Federalism (A Fifty Years of Political and Historical Portrait of Ethiopia). A Participant-Observer Perspective*. Ph.D. Thesis, Troy.

Ayana, Daniel (2010) "The 'Galla' That Never Was: Its Origin and Reformulation in a Hinterland of Comparative Disadvantage." *Journal of Oromo Studies*, 17 (1), 1–40.

Basuyau, Vincent (1991) *Le chemin de fer de Djibouti à Addis Abeba*. Mémoire de DEA, Université de Paris I-Panthéon-Sorbonne.

Bauer, Gretchen and Scott D. Taylor (2005) *Politics in Southern Africa: State and Society in Transition*. London: Lynne Rienner Publishers.

Baxter, Peter W. T., Jan Hultin, and Alessandro Triulzi (eds.) (1996) *Being and Becoming Oromo: Historical and Anthropological Enquiries*. Uppsala: Nordiska Afrikainstitutet.

Behadad, Ali (1994) *Belated Travelers: Orientalism in the Age of Colonial Dissolution*. Durham and London: Duke University Press.

Beke, Charles T. (1843) "On the Countries South of Abyssinia." *Journal of the Royal Geographical Society of London*, 13, 254–269.

Bernard, Marius (1872) *Quelques considérations sur les rétentions d'urine dans les lésions et les affections du système nerveux*. Paris: L. Cristin.

Bernard, Marius (1882) *Constitution médicale de Cannes pendant l'année 1881–1882. note sur la fièvre typhoïde*. Paris: Impr. De L. Vincent.

Bernard, Marius (1885) *De Toulon au Tonkin*. Paris: Laplace.

Bernard, Marius (1892) *De Tripoli à Tunis*. Paris: Librairie Renouard.

Bernet, Edmond (1912) *En Tripolitaine, voyage à Ghadamès*. Paris: Fontemoing.

Bertholon, Lucien and Chantre Ernest (1912–1913) *Recherches anthropologiques dans la Berbérie orientale: Tripolitaine, Tunisie, Algérie*. Lyon: A. Rey, vol. I: Anthropométrie, craniométrie, ethnographie.

Blanc, Édouard (1890) *Les routes de l'Afrique septentrionale au Soudan*. Paris: Société de géographie.

Boahen, Adu (1990) *African Perspectives on Colonialism*. Baltimore: Johns Hopkins University Press.

Bonner, Phillip (2002) *Kings, Commoners, and Concessionaires: The Evolution and Dissolution of the Nineteenth-century Swazi State*. Cambridge: Cambridge University Press.

Boonet, Cecile (1977) *Le Ruanda-Urundi: Naissance et Organisation d'un Territoire à Mandat*. Dissertation, Groupe: Histoire, Faculté de Philosophie et Lettres, Université Libre de Bruxelles.

Booth, Alan R. (2000) *Historical Dictionary of Swaziland*. Second Edition. Lanham: Scarecrow Press.

Boubacar, Barry (1998) *Senegambia and the Atlantic Slave Trade*. Cambridge: Cambridge University Press.

Bradbury, Mark (2008) *Becoming Somaliland*. London: James Currey.

Bradbury, Mark, Adan Yusuf Abokor, and Haroon Ahmed Yusuf (2003) "Somaliland: Choosing Politics Over Violence." *Review of African Political Economy*, 30 (97), 455–478.

Brass, Jennifer N. (2008) "Djibouti's Unusual Resource Course." *Journal of Modern African Studies*, 46 (4), 523–545.

Brons, Maria (2001) *Society, Security, Sovereignty and the State in Somalia: From Statelessness to Statelessness?* Utrecht: International Books.

Brooks, George (1975) "Peanuts and Colonialism: Consequences of the Commercialization of Peanuts in West Africa, 1830–1870." *Journal of African History*, 16 (30), 29–54.

Burgwyn, H. James (1997) *Italian Foreign Policy in the Interwar Period, 1918–1940*. London: Praeger Publishers.

Byrnes, Rita (ed.) (1996) *South Africa: A Country Study*. Washington, DC: PO for the Library of Congress.

Cain, P. J. and A. G. Hopkins (2016) *British Imperialism 1688–2015*. Oxon: Routledge.

Calchi Novati, Giampaolo (2009) "Colonialism as State-Maker in the History of the Horn of Africa: A Reassessment." In: *Proceedings of the 16th International Conference of Ethiopian Studies*, ed. by Svein Ege, Harald Aspen, Birhanu Teferra and Shiferaw Bekele. Trondheim: NTNU.

Carroll, Anthony J. and B. Rajagopal (1993) "The Case for the Independent Statehood of Somaliland." *American University Journal of International Law and Policy*, 8 (2/3), 653–681.

Castagno, Margaret (1975) *Historical Dictionary of Somalia*. Metuchen: The Scarecrow Press.

Caulk, Richard A. (1978) "Armies as Predators: Soldiers and Peasants in Ethiopia, ca. 1850–1935." *International Journal of African Historical Studies*, 11 (3), 457–493.

Caulk, Richard A. (2002) *"Between the Jaws of Hyenas": A Diplomatic History of Ethiopia (1876–1896)*. Wiesbaden: Harrassowitz.

Cecchi, Antonio (1886) *Da Zeila alle Frontiere del Caffa*. Roma: Ermanno Loescher and Co.

Ibid. Centre des Archives diplomatiques de Nantes (CADN).

Chabal, Patrick and Jean-Pascal Daloz (1999) *Africa Works: Disorder as Political Instrument*. Oxford: Oxford University Press.

Chafer, Tony (2002) *The End of Empire in French West Africa: France's Successful Decolonization?* Oxford: Oxford University Press.

Chamberlain, Joseph (1897) "The True Conception of Empire." In: *The Worlds Famous Orations*, vol. V.

Chamberlain, M. E. (2013) *The Scramble for Africa*. London: Routledge.

Chanie, Paulos (1998) "The Rise of Politicized Ethnicity Among the Oromo in Ethiopia." In: *Ethnicity and the State in Eastern Africa*, ed. by M. A. Mohamed Salih and John Markakis. Uppsala: Nordiska Afrikainstitutet.

Chrétien, Jean-Pierre (2003) *The Great Lakes of Africa: Two Thousand Years of History*. Cambridge, MA: The MIT Press.

Clément, José (2006) "Le Ruanda-Urundi et la Tutelle Belge." In: *La colonisation belge. Une grande aventure*, ed. by Gérard Jacques et al. Bruxelles: Blanchart.

Constant, Espoumel de and Paul-Henri-Benjamin Balluet (1891) *La politice française en Tunisie; le protectorat et ses origines (1854–1891)*. Paris: Paris E. Plon, Nourrit.

Constitution of the Republic of Somaliland (2001). Available online: www.somalilandlaw.com (accessed 20.8.2014).

Crummey, Donald (2000) *Land and Society in the Christian Kingdom of Ethiopia: From the Thirteenth to the Twentieth Century*. Urbana and Chicago: University of Illinois Press.

Daly, M. W. (1991) *Imperial Sudan: The Anglo-Egyptian Condominium 1934–1956*. Cambridge: Cambridge University Press.

Darkwah, R. H. Kofi (1975) *Shewa, Menelik and the Ethiopian Empire 1813–1889*. London: Oxford University Press.

Depelchin, Jacques (1992) *From the Congo Free State to Zaire (1885–1974): Towards a Demystification of Economic and Political History*. London: Codesria.

Eldredge, Elizabeth A. (2002) *A South African Kingdom: The Pursuit of Security in Nineteenth-century Lesotho*. New York: Cambridge University Press.

Epstein, Mortimer (ed.) (1928) *The Statesman's Year-Book: Statistical and Historical Annual of the States of the World for the Year 1928*. London: Macmillan and Co.

Etefa, Tsega (2013) *Integration and Peace in East Africa: A History of the Oromo Nation*. New York: Palgrave Macmillan.

Farley, Benjamin R. (2010) "Calling a State a State: Somaliland and International Recognition." *Emory International Law Review*, 24 (2), 777–820.

Ferguson, Niall (2004) *Empire: How Britain Made the Modern World*. London: Penguin Books.

Foureau, Fernand (1986) *Dans le grand Erg, mes itinéraires sahariens de décembre 1895 à mars 1896: rapport adressé à M. le ministre de l'instruction publique, à M. le gouverneur de l'Algérie, à l'Académie des inscriptions et belles-lettres*. Paris: A. Challamel.

Friedrichsmeyer, Sara, Sara Lennox, and Susanne Zantop (eds.) (1998) *The Imperialism Imagination: German Colonialism and Its Legacy*. Ann Arbor: University of Michigan Press.

Frileuze de, Henri (1900) *Impressions de voyage: Algérie et Tunisie*. Alençon: Impr. De A. Manier.

Gascon, Alain (2006) "Fin du chemin de fer, fin de Grande Éthiopie. La mort annoncée du chemin de fer de Menilek." In: *Le chemin de fer en Afrique*, ed. by J. L. Chaleard, C. Chanson-Jabeur and C. Béranger. Paris: Karthala, 35–54.

Gebissa, Ezekiel (2004) *Leaf of Allah: Khat and Agricultural Transformation in Hararghe, Ethiopia (1875–1991)*. Oxford: James Currey.

Geschekter, Charles (1997) "The Death of Somalia in Historical Perspective." In: *Mending Rips in the Sky: Options for Somali Communities in the 21st Century*, ed. by Hussein M. Adan and Richard Ford. Trenton, NJ: The Red Sea Press, 65–98.

Gharipour, Mohammad and Nilay Özlü (2015) *The City in the Muslim World: Depictions by Western Travel Writers*. London: Routledge.

Gillis, Hugh (1999) *The Kingdom of Swaziland: Studies in Political History*. Westport: Greenwood Press.

Glass, Harol M. (1966) *South African Policy Towards Basutoland*. Johannesburg: The South African Institute of International Affairs.

Gnamo, Abbas H. (2014) *Conquest and Resistance in the Ethiopian Empire, 1880–1974: The Case of Arsi Oromo*. Leiden: Brill.

Gondola, Ch. Didier (2002) *The History of Congo*. Westport: Greenwood Publishing Group.

Gray, John M. (1966) *History of the Gambia*. London: Frank Class.

Hameso, Seyoum and Mohammed Hassen (eds.) (2006) *Arrested Development in Ethiopia*. Trenton, NJ: The Red Sea Press.

Harroy, Jean-Paul (1984) *Rwanda. De la Féodalité á la Démocratie 1955–1962*. Bruxelles: Hayez.

Havinden, Michael and David Meredith (1993) *Colonialism and Development: Britain and Its Tropical Colonies 1850–1960*. London: Routledge.

Hesse-Wartegg de, Ernst (1882) *Tunis – The Land and the People*. New York: Dodd, Mead, and Company.

Höhne, Marcus V. (2006) "Political Identity, Emerging State Structures and Conflict in Northern Somalia." *Journal of Modern African Studies*, 44 (3), 397–414.

Hughes, Arnold and David Perfect (2008) *A Political History of the Gambia, 1816–1994*. Rochester: University of Rochester Press.

Hyam, Ronald (1972) *The Failure of South African Expansion 1908–1948*. London: Palgrave Macmillan Press.

Iggers, George (1997) "From Macro-to Microhistory: The History of Everyday Life." In: *Historiography of the 20th Century*. Hanover: Wesleyan University Press, published by University Press of New England.

Imbert-Vier, Simon (2011) *Traces des frontières à Djibouti. Des territoires et des hommes aux XIXe et XXe siècles*. Paris: Karthala.

Jacques, Gérard (1995) *Lualaba. Histoires de l'Afrique profonde*. Bruxelles: Racine.

Jalata, Asafa (2009) "Being in and Out of Africa. The Impact of Duality of Ethiopianism." *Journal of Black Studies*, 40 (2), 189–214.

Jalata, Asafa (2010) *Contending Nationalisms of Oromia and Ethiopia: Struggling for Statehood, Sovereignty, and Multinational Democracy*. Binghamton: Global Academic Publishing.

Jhazbhay, Iqbal (2009) *Somaliland: An African Struggle for Nationhood and International Recognition*. Institute for Global Dialogue and South African Institute of International Affairs.

Johnson, Robert (2003) *British Imperialism*. New York: Palgrave Macmillan.

Kinigi, Firmin (1971) *Realisations économiques de la Belgique au Rwanda et au Burundi pendant les vingt premiéres anées de son administraton (1920–1940)*. Louvain: Université Catholique de Louvain.

Küng, Heribert (2003) *Staatsminister Alfred Ilg (1854–1916), ein Thurgauer am Hof Kaiser Menelik II. von Äthiopien*. Thesis-Verl., Zürich, 1999.; *Alfred Ilg – Der weiße Abessinier*, un film de Christoph Kühn. Suisse.

La Berge de, Albert (1881) *En Tunisie*. Paris: Firmin-Didot.

Lange, Matthew, James Mahoney, and Matthias von Hau (2006) "Colonialism and Development: A Comparative Analysis of Spanish and British Colonies." *American Journal of Sociology*, 111 (5), 1412–1462.

Law, Robin (ed.) (1995) *From Slave Trade to "Legitimate" Commerce: The Commercial Transition in Nineteenth-Century West Africa*. Cambridge: Cambridge University Press.

Lecocq, Baz (2010) *Disputed Desert: Decolonisation, Competing Nationalisms, and Tuareg Rebellions in Northern Mali*. Leiden: Brill.

Lehning, James R. (2013) *European Colonialism Since 1700*. New York: Cambridge University Press.

Leroy-Beaulieu, Paul (1887) *L'Algérie et la Tunisie*. Paris: Guillaumin.

Levi, Giovanni (1991) "On Microhistory." In: *New Perspectives on Historical Writing*, ed. by Peter Burke. University Park, PA: Pennsylvania State Press.

Lewis, David L. (1987) *The Race to Fashoda: European Colonialism and African Resistance in the Scramble for Africa*. New York: Weidenfeld and Nicholson.

Lewis, Ioan M. (1961) *A Pastoral Democracy: A Study of Pastoralism and Politics Among the Northern Somali of the Horn of Africa*. Oxford: Oxford University Press.

Lewis, Ioan M. (2003) *A Modern History of the Somali: Nation and State in the Horn of Africa*. Athens: Ohio University Press.

Lewis, Ioan M. (2010) *Making and Breaking States in Africa: The Somali Experience*. Trenton, NJ: The Red Sea Press.

Lorin, Henri (1896) *Une promenade en Tunisie*. Paris: Hachette.

Lorin, Henri (1986) "En Tunisie: Le port de Sfax." *Questions politiques et coloniales*, 1, 356.

Loth, Gaston (1907) *La Tunisie, l'oeuvre du protectorat français*. Paris: Librarie Ch. Delagrave.

Lowe, C. J. and F. Marzari (2001) *Italian Foreign Policy, 1870–1940*. London: Routledge.

Magagula, Petros Q. (1998) *Swaziland's Relations With Britain and South Africa Since 1968, Durham Theses*. Durham: Durham University Press.

Mahoney, Florence K. O. (1963) *Government and Opinion in the Gambia 1816–1901*. London: University of London.

Mamdani, Mahmood (1999) "Historicizing Power and Responses to Power: Indirect Rule and Its Reform." *Social Research*, 66 (3), 859–886.

Mann, Michael (2004) "Torchbearers Upon the Path of Progress. Britain's Ideology of a Moral and Material Progress in India. An Introductory Essay." In: *Colonialism as Civilizing Mission: Cultural Ideology in British India*, ed. by H. Fischer-Tiné and M. Mann. London: Wimbledon Publishing Company.

Manning, Patrick (1998) *Francophone Sub-Saharan Africa 1880–1995*. Cambridge: Cambridge University Press.

Marcus, Harold G. (1992) "The Corruption of Ethiopian History." In: *Proceedings of the Sixth Michigan State University Conference on Northeast Africa*, compiled by John T. Hinnant and Beth Finne. East Lansing: Michigan State University.

Markakis, John (2011) *Ethiopia: The Last Two Frontiers*. Woodbridge: James Currey.

Marks, Thomas A. (1974) "Djibouti: France's Strategic Toehold in Africa." *African Affairs*, 73 (290), 95–104.

Mashasha, F. J. (1974) *The Swazi and Land Partition (1902–1910)*. Collected Seminar Papers, Institute of Commonwealth Studies, 17, 87–107.

Mbogoni, Lawrence E. Y. (1998) *The Cross vs. The Crescent. Religion and Politics in Tanzania: From the 1890s to the 1990s*. Dar es Salaam: Mkuki na Nyota Publishers.

McIntyre, David W. (2014) *Winding Up the British Empire in the Pacific Islands*. Oxford: Oxford University Press.

Melbaa, Gadaa (1988) *Oromia: An Introduction*. Khartoum: Goverment Printer.

Menkhaus, Ken (1997) "International Peacebuilding and the Dynamics of Local and National Reconciliation in Somalia." In: *Learning From Somalia: The Lessons of Armed Humanitarian Intervention*, ed. by Walter Clarke and Jeffrey Herbst. Boulder: Westview Press, 42–63.

Menkhaus, Ken (2000) "Traditional Conflict Management in Contemporary Somalia." In: *Traditional Cures for Modern Conflicts: African Conflict "Medicine,"* ed. by I. William Zartman. London: Lynne Rienner Publishers, 183–199.

Meredith, Martin (2008) *Diamonds, Gold and War: The British, the Boers, and the Making of South Africa*. New York: Simon & Schuster.

Michel, Léon (1867) *Tunis : l'orient africain, arabes, maures, kabyles, juifs, levantins, scènes de moeurs, intérieurs maures et israélites* . . . Paris: Garnier frères.

Milkias, Paulos and Getachew Metaferia (ed.) (2005) *The Battle of Adowa: Reflections on Ethiopia's Historic Victory Against European Colonialism.* New York: Algora Publishing.

Millet, René (1913) *La conquête du Maroc; La question indigène (Algérie et Tunisie).* Paris: Perrin.

Mohamoud, Abdullah A. (2006) *State Collapse and Post-Conflict Development in Africa: The Case of Somalia (1960–2001).* West Lafayette, IN: Purdue University Press.

Montet, Édouard (1903) *Voyage au Maroc.* Paris: Reprod. D'un extrait du Tour du monde, 29–36, 337–432.

Morton, Fred, Jeff Ramsay, and Part T. Mgadla (2008) *Historical Dictionary of Botswana.* Lanham: Scarecrow Press.

Mouser, Bruce (1971) *Government and Opinion in the Gambia 1816–1901.* Bloomington, IN: Indiana University Press.

Ndaywel É Nziem, Isidore (1998) *Congo. De l'héritage ancien à la République Démocratique.* Paris: Duculot.

Negash, Tekeste (1990) *The Crisis of Ethiopian Education.* Uppsala: Uppsala University.

Newbury, David (1991) *Kings and Clans: Ijwi Island and the Lake Kivu Rift, 1780–1840.* Madison: University of Wisconsin Press.

New Trouble for French Colony on Red Sea, *MERIP Reports*, No. 45m 1976, 22.

Nsanze, Augustin (1980) *Un Domaine Royal au Burundi. Mbuye (env. 1850–1945).* Bujumbura: Société Française d'Histoire des Outre-Mers.

Nsanze, Augustin (2001) *Le Burundi Ancien. L'économie du Pouvoir de 1875 à 1920.* Paris: L'Harmattan.

Nsanze, Augustin (2003) *Le Burundi Contemporain. L'État-nation en question (1956–2002).* Paris: L'Harmattan.

Nugent, Paul (2004) *Africa Since Independence.* New York: Palgrave Macmillan.

Nyambariza, Daniel (1990) "A Demographic Approach to Colonial Burundi, From Administrative Documents, 1896–1960." In: *Demography From Scanty Evidence: Central Africa in the Colonial Era*, ed. by Bruce Fetter. Boulder and London: Lynne Rienner Publishers, 101–113.

Oliver Roland and G. N. Sanderson (eds.) (1985) *The Cambridge History of Africa: Volume 6 From 1870 to 1905.* Cambridge: Cambridge University Press.

Olson, James and Robert Shadle (eds.) (1996) *Historical Dictionary of the British Empire.* Westport: K-Z. Westport: Greenwood Press.

Osman, Abdulahi A. (2007) "Cultural Diversity and the Somali Conflict: Myth or Reality?" *African Journal on Conflict Resolution*, 7 (2), 93–134.

Østebø, Terje (2008) "The Question of Becoming: Islamic Reform Movements in Contemporary Ethiopia." *Journal of Religion in Africa*, 38 (4), 416–446.

Pankhurst, Richard (1997) *The Ethiopian Borderlands: Essays in Regional History From Ancient Times to the End of the 18th Century.* Lawrenceville and Asmara: The Red Sea Press.

Parsons, Neil (1982) *King Khama Emperor Joe and the Great White Queen Victorian Britain Through African Eyes*. Chicago: The University of Chicago Press.

Penner, C. D. (1940) "Germany and the Transvaal Before 1896." *Journal of Modern History*, 12 (1), 31–58.

Peyssonnel, Jean-André (1838) *Voyages dans les Régences de Tunis et d'Alger*. Paris: Gide, 2 vol. (t. 1 Relation d'un voyage sur les côtes de Barbarie, fait par ordre du Roi en 1724 et 1725).

Plowden, Walter Ch. (1868) *Travels in Abyssinia and the Galla Country*. London: Longman, Green, and Co.

Potholm, Christian (1993) *Swaziland: The Dynamics of Political Modernization*. Berkeley: University of California Press.

Prijac, Lukian (2003) *Antony Klobukowski et le traité franco-éthiopien de 1908*. Paris: Aresæ.

Proctor, J. H. (1973) "Traditionalism and Parliamentary Government in Swaziland." *African Affairs*, 72 (288), 273–287.

Pugh, Martin (1999) *Britain Since 1789: A Concise History*. Hampshire: Macmillan Press.

Putnam, Aric (2007) "Ethiopia Is Now: J.A. Rogers and the Rhetoric of Black Anti-colonialism During the Great Depression." *Rhetoric and Public Affairs*, 10 (3), 419–444.

Pyeatt, Duane N. (1998) *Heligoland and the Making of the Anglo-German Colonial Agreement in 1890: A Thesis in History*. Lubbock: Texas Tech University.

Ramsbotham, Oliver and Tom Woodhouse (2013) *Peacekeeping and Conflict Resolution*. London: Routledge.

Roethke, Peter (2011) "The Right to Secede Under International Law: The Case of Somaliland." *Journal of International Service*, 20 (2), 35–48.

Rosenberg, Scott and Richard F. Weisfelder (2013) *Historical Dictionary of Lesotho*. Iahman: Scarecrow Press.

Rouaud, Alain (1997) "Pour une histoire des Arabes de Djibouti, 1896–1977." *Cahiers d'études africaines*, 37 (146), 319–348.

Rubenson, Sven (1991) *The Survival of Ethiopian Independence*. Addis Ababa: Kuraz Publishing Agency.

Rubinkowska, Hanna (2010) *Ethiopia on the Verge of Modernity: The Transfer of Power During Zewditu's Reign 1916–1930*. Warsaw: Wydawnictwo AGADE.

Rudakemwa, Fortunatus (2005) *L'évangelisation du Rwanda*. Paris: L'Harmattan.

Sarkin, Jeremy (2011) *Germany's Genocide of the Herero: Kaiser Wilhelm II., His General, His Settlers, His Soldiers*. Cape Town: UCT Press.

Schlee, Günther (2003) "Redrawing the Map of the Horn: The Politics of Difference." *Africa*, 73 (3), 343–368.

Schmitt, Deborah A. (2006) *The Bechuanaland Pionners and Gunners*. Westport: Praeger Publishers.

Schnee, Heinrich (1926) *German Colonization: Past and Future – The Truth About the German Colonies*. New York: Alfred A. Knopf.

Schraeder, Peter J. (1993) "Ethnic Politics in Djibouti: From 'Eye of the Hurricane' to 'Boiling Cauldron'." *African Affairs*, 92 (367), 203–221.

Shell, Robert C. H. (2000) "Islam in Southern Africa, 1652–1998." In: *The History of Islam in Africa*, ed. by Nehemia Levtzion and Randall L. Pouwels. Oxford: James Currey, 327–348.

Simone, E. (1973) "The Amhara Military Expeditions Against the Shawa Galla (1800–1850): A Reappraisal." In: *Proceedings of the First United States Conference on Ethiopian Studies, 1973*. East Lansing: Michigan State University.

Smith, Lahra (2014) *Making Citizens in Africa: Ethnicity, Gender, and National Identity in Ethiopia*. Cambridge: Cambridge University Press.

Springhall, Jason (2001) *Decolonization Since 1945*. New York: Palgrave.

Ssereo, Florence (2003) "Clanpolitics, Clan-democracy and Conflict Regulation in Africa: The Experience of Somalia." *Global Review of Ethnopolitics*, 2 (3–4), 25–40.

Stengers, Jean (1989) *Congo mythes et réalités. 100 and d'histoire*. Paris: Duculot.

Stumme, Hans (1900) *Märchen der Berbern von Tamazratt*. Leipzig.

Styan, David (2013) *Djibouti: Challenging Influence in the Horn's Strategic Hub*. Chatham House Briefing Paper, AFP BP 2013/01, 5.

Swindell, Kenneth and Alieu Jeng (2006) *Migrants, Credit and Climate: The Gambian Groundnut Trade, 1834–1934*. Leiden: Brill.

Teka, Tegegne (1998) "Amhara Ethnicity in the Making." In: *Ethnicity and the State in Eastern Africa*, ed. by M. A. Mohamed Salih and John Markakis. Uppsala: Nordiska Afrikainstitutet.

Thompson, Gardner (2003) *Governing Uganda: British Colonial Rule and Its Legacy*. Kampala: Fountain Publisher.

Touval, Saadia (1963) *Somali Nationalism: International Politics and the Drive for Unity in the Horn of Africa*. Cambridge, MA: Harvard University Press.

Trapido, Stanely and Ian Phimister (2008) "Imperialism, Settler Identities and Colonial Capitalism: The Hundred Year Origins of the 1899 South African War." *Historia*, 53 (1), 43–75.

Tripodi, Paolo (1999) *The Colonial Legacy in Somalia: Rome and Mogadishu: From Colonial Administration to Operation Restore Hope*. New York: Palgrave Macmillan.

Vandervort, Bruce (1998) *Wars of Imperial Conquest in Africa 1830–1914*. London and New York: Routledge.

Van Gelder Pineda de, Rosanna (1995) *Le Chemin de fer de Djibouti à Addis-Abeba*. Paris: L'Harmattan.

Van Walraven, Klaas (2013) *The Yearning for Relief: A History of the Sawaba Movement in Niger*. Leiden: Brill.

Walker, A. (ed.) (1963) *The Cambridge History of the British Empire. Vol. VIII: South Africa, Rhodesia, and the High Commission Territories*. New York: Cambridge University Press.

Walker, E. A. and L. Harlech (1945) "The British South African Territories." *African Affairs*, 44 (175), 62–73.

Yasin, Mohammed Yasin (2010) "Trans-Border Political Alliance in the Horn of Africa: The Case of the Afar-Issa Conflict." In: *Borders and Borderlands as Resources in the Horn of Africa*, ed. by Dereje Feyissa and Markus Virgil Hoehne. Oxford: James Currey, 88–89.

Young, Crawford (2007) "Nation, Ethnicity, and Citizenship: Dilemmas of Democracy and Civil Order in Africa." In: *Making Nations, Creating Strangers: States and Citizenship in Africa*, ed. by Sarah Dorman, Daniel Hammett and Paul Nugent. Leiden: Brill.

Zartman, William I. (ed.) (2000) *Traditional Cures for Modern Conflicts: African Conflict "Medicine."* London: Lynne Rienner Publishers.

Zewde, Bahru (2001) *A History of Modern Ethiopia, 1885–1991.* Oxford: James Currey.

Zewde, Bahru (2002) *Pioneers of Change in Ethiopia: The Reformist Intellectuals of the Early Twentieth Century.* Oxford: James Currey.

Zewde, Bahru (2008) "The City Centre: A Shifting Concept in the History of Addis Ababa." In: *Society, State, and History: Selected Essays.* ed. by Bahru Zewde. Addis Ababa: Addis Ababa University Press.

Zins, Henryk (1997) "The International Context of the Creation of the Bechuanaland Protectorate in 1885." *PULA Journal of African Studies*, 11 (1), 54–62.

Index